Santa Clara County Free Library

This book may be kept 14 days.

A fine of 5 cents per day will be charged
on books kept overtime.

No books will be issued to persons in
arrears for fines.

Books must not be loaned by the borrower.

Careful usage of books is expected, and any soiling,
injury, or loss is to be paid for by the borrower.

CHALLENGE OF THE UNKNOWN

Sir Edmund Hillary *(The Times, London)*

CHALLENGE
OF THE
UNKNOWN

EDITED BY

SIR EDMUND HILLARY

illustrated with photographs

E. P. D   ORK

INDIVIDUAL COPYRIGHTS

CONTENTS

7

ILLUSTRATIONS

FOREWORD

BY SIR EDMUND HILLARY

In October 1956 a two-engined DC3 aircraft of the United States Navy flew from its base in McMurdo Sound into the region of the South Pole. While its escorting plane, a giant four-engined Globemaster, circled overhead, the DC3 made several low level flights over the ten thousand foot plateau and then gently touched down on the firm surface in a cloud of powder snow. The first landing by aircraft on the South Pole had been achieved and the first men stood on the pole since Captain Scott and his small band. Six hours later the successful crew were celebrating their achievement back in the warmth and comfort of their base.

What a different story it was in 1912 when Scott reached the Pole. Despite great physical discomfort, Scott and his men with almost superhuman strength and determination dragged their laden sledge up the Beardmore glacier and for day after day across the cold, windswept polar plateau. They arrived at the South Pole only to find that Amundsen, the great Norwegian explorer had reached it before them. How bitter their disappointment must have been. Yet their journey was only half over. They still had to get home. Their epic trip back over the Beardmore glacier and across the vast expanse of the Ross Ice shelf has written a glorious page in the history of British exploration. They died only a few short miles from safety but their courage and endurance are still an inspiration to all of those who are prepared to gamble hardship and

9

discomfort, and perhaps even life itself, against the achieving of a worthwhile aim in the unexplored corners of the globe.

Modern developments in machinery and equipment have produced major changes in the technique of exploration. Aircraft and vehicles are in many cases replacing the human legs; oxygen bottles are giving new strength to air-starved lungs in the thin air that clothes the giants of the Himalayas; and radio communication has removed the loneliness from the most desolate land. But despite all this I firmly believe that in the end it is the man himself that counts. When the going gets tough and things go wrong the same qualities are needed to win through as they were in the past—qualities of courage, resourcefulness, the ability to put up with discomfort and hardship, and the enthusiasm to hold tight to an ideal and to see it through with doggedness and determination.

The explorers of the past were great men and we should honour them. But let us not forget that their spirit still lives on. It is still not hard to find a man who will adventure for the sake of a dream or one who will search, for the pleasure of searching, and not for what he may find.

Publisher's Note

The grammatical usage and styling of each source have been maintained, as closely as possible, in the present selections.

CHALLENGE OF THE UNKNOWN

RALPH IZZARD

THE PURSUIT OF THE YETI

(From THE ABOMINABLE SNOWMAN. New York: Doubleday & Co., Inc., 1955)

The truth about the 'Yeti' or 'Abominable Snowman' is still unknown, and if he is finally proved to be a bear or an ape, many people will be sorry—there are so few mysteries left. In 1954, Ralph Izzard and Tom Stobart set out to solve this one. With them went Charles Stonor, biologist and anthropologist, Gerald Russell, big game hunter, John Jackson, and Bill Edgar as doctor. Tom Stobart was a member of the Everest Team, and Izzard had been with our 1953 Everest Expedition. Here is Izzard's account of some of the many false Yeti trails followed.

Tom Stobart took on the immense task of ordering and assembling our equipment and stores. Anyone who had not had his considerable experience of expedition work would have thrown up the task as hopeless. We had been forced to put back the sailing date of the main party to December 30th, when accommodation had been booked in the P. and O. liner *Strathaird,* but Messrs. Andrew Lusk of Wapping who had been engaged to pack, crate and dispatch our requirements, informed us that, owing to the Christmas holidays, everything must be in their warehouses by December 12th at the latest. This gave us barely three weeks in which to assemble between six and seven tons of assorted goods. Tents had not only to be ordered, they had to be made. The same applied to climbing boots and high-altitude clothing. It is impossible to list the thousand and one separate items which had to be thought of. In 'hardware' it ranged from ammunition and Very lights and pistols for signalling, to traps of all sizes, to

13

wire and wire-netting, right down to the humble darning needle. 'Soft goods' included mosquito netting, nets for hunting, lightweight tarpaulins and polythene bags of all sizes, including one huge one labelled 'Abominable Snowman' in case we came across a dead specimen. Tom paid particular attention to food. A magnificent cook himself, he has very decided opinions as to what expeditions should be expected to eat while undertaking strenuous work at high altitude and, with the aid of Dr. Griffith Pugh, physiologist with Sir John Hunt's Everest team, he worked out a special diet for us. One can, I think, say confidently that no Himalayan expedition has ever eaten better, and to this we largely attribute the fact that our expedition was almost entirely free from illness.

Round Danu's preposterously large campfire that evening morale was higher than it had ever been. We drank two bottles of rum on the strength of it—rather reckless extravagance, the ration to which we had restricted ourselves being one bottle of spirits per week among the nine of us. Counting Stonor's discovery, we had now found Yeti tracks at two distinct points in the area we were trying to cover. The points were many miles apart and separated by tremendous mountain barriers. It seemed that the Yeti might not be so thin on the ground as we had supposed. We finished the evening with a balalaika concert at which Gerald was the star performer.

The next day was a busy one. I sat down to write a five 'take' story for the *Daily Mail* recounting the experiences of John's party, and those of ourselves under Charles. Tom, who is something of an artist, obliged with a drawing of the Yeti which he made by following the instructions of a number of over-critical Sherpas who would not accept it as authentic until they had made a number of alterations and additions. John drew a sketch-map of the area, which already contained many corrections of the maps which we had brought with us. All this material with the several rolls of films made an excellent 'bag' for the next runner to take back to Katmandu. In the afternoon we posed for a group picture wearing our windproof suits with their various dazzling colours. These colours were chosen not only because they were aesthetically cinematic, but because they helped us to recognize each other at a distance. But after our first sortie we had already become dubious about the policy of wearing bright garments, for on the vast bare snow slopes it had become apparent we should be quite conspicuous enough to a Yeti without parading about in clothes more suited to a harlequin. From then on most of our work was done in drab, or khaki, clothes except when it was imperative to protect ourselves from bad weather.

That night we had our second council of war and decided to re-form our previous search parties. A glance at the map will show that the three river valleys of the Bhote Kosi, the Dudh Kosi and the Chola Khola run roughly parallel and are separated by mountain ranges which are never less than 18,000 feet and carry peaks like Taweche which is over 21,000 feet high. The three valleys terminate to the north at the foot of an even higher lateral range, which marks the Tibetan Frontier and which is straddled by giants like Cho Oyu and Gyachung Kang, both of them about 26,000 feet high. To the best of our knowledge the ranges had only once been crossed from the upper Bhote Kosi to the upper Dudh Kosi valley and only once from the Chola Khola to the Dudh Kosi. This last crossing was accomplished last year by Hillary, Noyce, Ward and Wiley of the British Everest Expedition, as strong a climbing team as is likely to be found in the world. Charles Stonor was still convinced that it would be possible to cross from the Dudh Kosi to the Bhote Kosi over the col at the head of the lateral Macherma valley which he and I had attempted until we found ourselves submerged almost up to the neck in deep powder snow. He was anxious now to go back to the Bhote Kosi and try the col from the opposite side. My own ambition was to push on beyond Macherma, up the Dudh Kosi to the Dudh Pokhari which I reckoned to be about four days' march from the Base Camp.

I have previously written in my dispatches that it was a 'hunch' which prompted this decision. It has, however, always been my experience that all sorts of animals find a single isolated lake an irresistible attraction, whether it be frozen or not. Charles and I therefore decided to part company, with reluctance on my part, for as well as on our first sortie, we had been companions for many months together in other parts of the Himalaya. He had however taught me enough to ensure that I could carry on efficiently alone. John Jackson and Stanley Jeeves were both anxious to go back to the Chola Khola Valley and the Khumbu Glacier where they had sighted the Yeti tracks. Tom Stobart with Bill Edgar and Chunk Lagus were now also ready to join the search and we decided that they should at first leave with Jackson and Jeeves and should later break away and explore the lower, eastern, side of Taweche mountain, where there had been plenty of Sherpa evidence of the recent presence of Yeti. Bis wished to spend a few days sorting out his equipment at the Base Camp in preparation for the collection of birds and mammals he was hoping to make. It was decided that when he was ready to leave he would join Charles Stonor up the Bhote Kosi. Gerald Russell decided to go with me. Thus the second sortie developed into a three-pronged drive up the three parallel valleys with the possibility that it might become a pincer movement from the centre valley either towards the east or towards the west.

This time we were all to take our Marconi walkie-talkie sets in the hope that we would be able to keep in touch with each other. If prints were found it was left to each party to decide whether a general "Tallyho" should be sounded to call everyone to one valley. The important point to be remembered was that it might be useless to call the entire team to tracks which were three or four days old. In doing so there was the danger that some of us would be drawn away from an area where a Yeti might be at the present time merely to a place where it had been some time ago in the past. It was agreed that we should all take enough food to stay out three weeks if necessary.

We had now begun our collection of wild animals with a stone marten and a mouse hare. The mouse hare—a perfect miniature of the common hare which would be an ideal children's pet if it could acclimatize itself to low altitudes— proved quite tame immediately on capture, so tame in fact that we felt that we might even shortly be able to give it the freedom of the camp. The stone marten, a most beautiful animal with thick grey-brown fur and blue eyes, remained ferocity itself from the day it was captured until it escaped some weeks later. It was caught in remarkable circumstances by Bahadur, a sixteen-year-old Katmandu coolie who had decided to remain behind as assistant cook to Narayan. Bahadur spotted the marten among some rocks near the kitchen and grabbed it with his bare hands. Impressed by its docility on this single occasion Ahkey Bhutia subsequently tried to handle it and was bitten severely in the finger for his temerity.

The next day, Saturday, was spent in sorting out food and equipment. This was the night of our big meal of the week and as we should not be eating together for some time Tom took over the cooking again; once more he excelled himself by producing *hors d'oeuvres* and lobster Newburg, using tinned salmon to supplement our small tinned lobster supply. There followed a magnificent chocolate cake baked by Narayan in Bis's tin collecting trunk and surmounted with an inch of whipped cream.

Next morning began with a screaming argument between Narayan and Ahkey which finished with Narayan in floods

of tears. This collapse delighted the arrogant Ahkey but
caused us much concern, for I for one knew that Narayan
had quite enough spirit in him to stick a kitchen knife in
Ahkey if he was goaded too far. It was therefore decided to
separate the two, Ahkey being left with Bis and Narayan
coming with me. My party was now made up of myself,
Gerald, Sirdar Ang Tschering, Narayan, Karma, another pro-
bationer cook whom Gerald persisted in calling "Little
Henry," Danu, Norbu, and nine coolies who included, by
special request, Gyalgen, known as the 'Jungli Sherpa'—he
was a local Sherpa who had been with us since Katmandu—
and his equally unkempt companion Ang Tilay. Ang Tilay
was quite the most uncouth Sherpa I have ever seen. Rag-
gedly dressed, incredibly dirty, with a rather shambling figure,
he balanced his shaggy head on top of an immense goitre.
But he was a gentle, kindly, great-hearted man and my affection and respect for him exceeded if anything my respect
and affection for the 'Jungli Sherpa.' Ang Tilay was tireless
in the chase and loped around the mountains like a casting
hound, covering in each day about three times more ground
than any of the rest of us. In spite of his appearance he was
a man of some substance and owned at least three houses,
including one at Nah about half-way up the Upper Dudh
Kosi Valley which he kept for the summer yak-grazing and
which was often to become our party's advance headquarters.
He knew the upper Dudh Kosi area intimately, claimed to
have seen a Yeti twice, had often heard the animal calling,
and had found tracks more often than he could remember.
He was thus an invaluable addition to my team.

As a chilly preliminary to our excursion I stripped to the
skin in the snow and washed from head to foot in a bucket
of hot water. A bath even in those Spartan conditions is a
luxury if one is not to enjoy another for three weeks. As
Gerald is the slower of the two of us, he decided to go on
ahead and we arranged that we should spend the night at

the woodcutter's cottage owned by the Brueghel family beyond Phorche village.

Snow had been falling intermittently all the week. When I left the Base Camp soon after lunch Gerald's tracks were already obliterated. We slithered down the path from the Base Camp to the Dudh Kosi river and then started the long climb up the Thyangboche spur towards the monastery. Where the path to Phorche branches off from the monastery track, snow was so heavy that I had difficulty in finding the beginning of the steep traverse above the Imja Khola river. As we brushed through the thicket, thick pads of damp snow, dislodged from the branches, fell onto our heads and down our necks.

My party had crossed the ice-covered bridge across the Imja Khola and had climbed about half-way up the Tahr Spur towards Phorche, when I was astonished to hear a distant shout behind us. This turned out to be Gerald, who I had thought by this time would be long past Phorche. But by mischance he had missed the turning where the Phorche pass leaves the Thyangboche track and had gone on almost up to the monastery. Here he was fortunately met by Sonam Tensing, known to many previous expeditions as 'the Foreign Sportsman,' who was on his way back to Phorche, his home village. The unfortunate Gerald was thus not only no longer ahead of us, but was back in his familiar position of about a mile behind and had climbed an extra thousand feet into the bargain. We pushed on to Phorche together, the snow still falling heavily, and made the customary halt for *chang* and *rakshi*, a fierce rice spirit.

Gerald and I passed only twenty minutes in Phorche before tackling the high traverse along the left bank of the Dudh Kosi. Monaul pheasants, as pretty as peacocks, scurried in the snow-laden undergrowth. Before we reached the cottage, which was to be our home for the night we also started droves of blood pheasants.

Once more the Brueghel family were only too delighted to evacuate their home and spend the night in Phorche in return for a lodging fee of one shilling for the house and provision fees of three shillings for eggs and three shillings for firewood. The Sherpas took up their quarters in the ground-floor stable normally reserved for Yaks, leaving Gerald and myself to occupy the first-floor living-room. This was not entirely a happy arrangement, for the pungent smoke from the yak-dung and damp juniper-bough fire which the Sherpas lit beneath us poured up through the cracks in the floor and nearly suffocated us before driving us once more into the open. As the snow had now stopped we decided to eat supper round a camp-fire on the small beaten earth platform beside the house. As it was six o'clock I now got out the walkie-talkie set and was delighted to find that we were in good clear contact with the Base Camp.

The clouds had now lifted and the peaks round us sparkled frostily in the moonlight high above the dark shadow of the fir trees. Danu's immense conflagration beneath our sleeping quarters had now been extinguished and, the dense smoke having cleared, we turned in at eight o'clock.

Next morning we were off to an early start, and after establishing brief radio contact with the Base Camp, continued up the left bank of the Dudh Kosi. Trailing in our wake was a party of woodcutters from Phorche, some of whom, being no more than eight years old, were scarcely as large as their carrying baskets. For the first mile the trail was almost hidden by snow and the locally recruited Sherpas and Sherpani porters, all of whom were wearing the local Tibetan-style felt boot, had difficulty in keeping to their feet. Once more we started up blood pheasants and also coveys of the giant Himalayan Snowcock. In spite of the worsened conditions both Gerald and I were going far better than on our first unacclimatized journey over the same route and made far better time on the frighteningly steep ascent up the right bank of the Dudh Kosi which leads from the water's edge to the yak-herds' huts at Dolle. Here we had hopes of interrogating the yak-herd who had discovered fresh Yeti tracks in the neighbourhood in the previous week. We found the hut deserted and learnt from a neighbour, who appeared to materialize from nowhere, that the owner would not be back until four o'clock that afternoon. The traverse along the right bank of the Dudh Kosi to Macherma is a long day's march however acclimatized one may be and we therefore decided that we must push on.

At Nub Gerald and I sat down to eat lunch beneath an immense rock outcrop which gave us a stupendous view down the valley to majestic Kangtega, superbly buttressed as it is by organ-pipe ice-fluting. A less welcome sight were banks of mist creeping up the valley behind us and already slowly hiding the trees above the Base Camp, which had still been visible to us. We therefore lost no time in pushing on, Gerald in his hurry leaving our only tin opener behind on the boulder which served us as a dining table. We reached our yak-herd's hut at Macherma just in advance of the swirling mist. Fuel was quite plentiful and we spent a comfortable evening round a pleasant fire of dwarf juniper boughs. At six o'clock I once more had radio contact with the Base Camp. But this time while I could hear them over their more powerful transmitter they could no longer hear me—a fact which caused me some uneasiness. Bis was speaking, from which I deduced that the other search parties had already set out from the camp. In spite of the fire, which we kept on replenishing, it turned out to be a bitterly cold night.

We were again up early the next morning and were filled with pleasant anticipations for, for the first time on this sortie, we would be breaking fresh ground. I had hoped that we might even go as far as Dudh Pokhari in the day, but it was soon apparent that this target would be well beyond us. In the early hours the mist had remained very thick and as the sun rose the mist did not lift with it. Our altitude was about 15,000 feet above the sea. It had begun to snow and the snow of the past few weeks had melted to nothing like the extent of that lower down the valley.

Before we started off I summoned Ang Tschering and told him to announce to everybody that I would pay a reward of 100 Nepali rupees (five pounds) to the first man or woman who discovered a genuine Yeti track. This was possibly a rash move for as it turned out I lost my money within twenty minutes. We turned the headland from the tiny village and had begun the steep traverse which continued up the right bank of the river, visibility being practically nil, when Ang Tschering, who had once more taken over the now arduous task of breaking the trail, suddenly stopped dead. We were half-way across a slope which lay in shadow so that the snow lay deeply. About six feet below our trail and now running parallel with it was a single line of tracks heading down the valley. They were quite distinct in spite of the snow which had fallen on them since they were made. We judged them to be about three days old. They were like nothing I had ever seen before. They still showed the clear imprint of one big toe and at least three smaller ones. Allowing for enlargement, we judged them to be eight or nine inches long and possibly four or five inches across. The stride could be accurately measured as uniformly two feet three inches long. Our general impression was that, although smaller, they corresponded exactly with those photographed by Eric Shipton in 1951. Both Gerald and I had no doubt whatever that they were those of a biped. Ang Tschering, possibly the most seasoned and experienced of all Sherpa sirdars, at once recognized them as Yeti and his opinion was immediately confirmed by Ang Tilay, who of all people knew what he was looking for, and by Danu and Norbu, who both claimed to have seen Yeti tracks previously. It was possibly unfortunate that the prize money was to go to Ang Tschering, who was the wealthiest

Sherpa with us. But the fact that none of the others questioned Ang Tschering's find and persisted in confirming it without any expectation of reward for themselves goes, I think, to prove the authenticity of the track.

The discovery of the footprints caused a good deal of excitement and uncertainty among the Sherpas. For some moments it was a case of those behind shouting "Forward" and those in front shouting "Back." The scene was an eerie one as we stood with wraiths of mist swirling about us, occasionally lifting so that we could see a hundred yards or so in any direction and then closing about us so that we could scarcely see each other. Going back on our tracks a little we got to the point where the Yeti, or whatever animal it was, had headed straight down the incline towards the river-bed. As the tracks were so old and must inevitably walk off the snow as they descended lower, we felt it would be more sensible to try and trace them back to their source. We thus continued along the traverse, the footprints keeping exactly parallel to our own path and six feet below it. After about three hundred yards our path led onto a small plateau which the animal had crossed confidently, but a few feet below the far rim of the plateau there was a confusion of marks, some being of the same size and others smaller. We first jumped to the conclusion that we must be dealing with a parent and child but we later came to believe that on approaching the new horizon of the plateau the creature—like any suspicious human being in similar circumstances—had dropped on all fours, the smaller indentations being its hands or knuckles, and had cautiously raised its head above the plateau to ensure that the coast was clear before advancing once more on its hind legs. The animal had approached the plateau by coming straight up from the river, meaning a difficult descent, and as the mist was closing down again we judged it imprudent to follow the trail further at that time. After a short distance our own path brought us to another uninhabited village and, pos-

sibly half a mile further on, to our delight, we again came
upon the tracks and obvious marks where the animal had sat
down in a number of positions upon a promontory, apparently observing the village closely before deciding on a deep
descending detour. The creature had clearly come down the
path we were now about to follow but for some time we were
disconcerted to see that the stride had visibly shortened while
there were many more footprints than there should have
been. We were reluctantly coming to the conclusion that we
were after all tracking a quadruped when to our relief and
encouragement the tracks suddenly divided round a boulder
leaving distinct marks of two bipeds walking possibly four
yards apart. The pattern of this track remained for a mile,
more often than not a single line, but occasionally dividing
to pass round either side of an obstruction. At one point a
wolf had crossed over the track at right angles, paused for an
obvious "double-take," and then returned to the tracks and
followed them for about ninety yards to satisfy its curiosity
before turning away again on its own errand. Finally, using
a dry water-course, the two tracks disappeared up the cliff to
our left, and there being little snow in this gully—while the
mist was now thickening dangerously—we abandoned them,
crossed the river to the left bank and bivouacked beside Ang
Tilay's house in the now empty yak-grazing village of Nah.

In retrospect, it was possibly a deciding factor in the failure of the ensuing pursuit that we remained fog-bound for
the rest of that day and during the early hours of the following morning. We thus had no chance to examine the surrounding country and make the best dispositions.

Next morning, shortly after we had resumed our march the
mist lifted, disclosing that the tracks had apparently come
from a vast amphitheatre high up the mountain-side, which
was filled with shattered boulders and glacier debris. We
were ruefully forming the opinion that this almost impenetrable hide-out must be the Yeti home, when a shout from

ahead announced that the tracks had again been sighted on the further bank of the river. Danu, with one of the younger Sherpas and myself, crossed the river by the precarious method of boulder-hopping and were immediately not in the least doubt that we were once more on the correct trail. Possibly the animals had made another detour to avoid Nah village, but it was now clear that their general route was down-river, using the yak ledges beneath the cliff and beside the water on the bank opposite to the main path. Dividing round boulders and uniting again where there were no obstructions the prints led upwards till at the foot of a steep waterfall, where the cliff rises sheer, the creatures had crossed to the left bank by means of a rough log bridge. A fiercely steep climb now brought us to the lake of Lang Boma upon which three ruddy sheldrake, their golden plumage glinting in the sun, were floating and beside which there was a positive maze of Yeti tracks as well as those of foxes, wolves and other animals.

When Gerald and I reached the Lang Boma we were too exhausted for the moment to do anything more than sit on a rock and gaze in bewilderment at the wealth of tracks before us. We were still not properly acclimatized and the last steep pitch had taxed us both severely. We had in fact been climbing steadily since Nah. The snow had been deep underfoot and beneath it the ground was covered with loose rocks and shale which made the going particularly heavy. For some time past Gerald had been able to do nothing but stick doggedly to the track. I was the stronger of the two of us but I had made a number of scrambling detours while following the footprints and was now fully as tired. Ang Tschering, who was still comparatively fresh, had, however, been casting round in an attempt to unravel the maze of Yeti tracks beside the lake. It was not long before he discovered a single distinct track approaching from the east. The find so excited him that I felt compelled to join him in the search, leaving Gerald still panting on his rock. Together we climbed the steep snow slope leading up to the lateral rim of the Dudh Kosi glacier and from this point through glasses we managed to pick out the track for over a mile as it led across the glacier in the general direction of Taweche peak and the great wall of rock and ice which separated our valley from the Chola Khola on the far side. The Yeti had not made a beeline across country but had carefully followed the contours of the snow slopes like any experienced tourist on skis. There was a kink on the top of our own slope—the kind of almost invisible hazard which sooner or later upsets all skiers—and, although on foot, I stumbled into it and pitched headlong into a snowdrift. On picking myself up I was amused to see that two yards to my right the Yeti had suffered exactly the same fate, but that after going headfirst into the drift it had avoided further catastrophe by squatting on its backside and tobogganing to the foot of the slope, using its fists on either side of its body to propel itself forwards and downwards. In doing so it had left a deep groove in the snow. (I have since been told on the best authority that it is a habit of gorillas to sit on their rumps and slide when descending steep banks.) At the end of its slide it had again risen to its feet and set off in its shambling gait, which now seemed to be a lurch forward on its toes.

Gerald had now recovered sufficiently to join in the tracking and it was he who discovered the footprints of a second Yeti leading down-river from the north. If anything, these tracks were fresher than those of the 'winter sports' Yeti and as they came from the direction in which we were now heading we decided to follow them. This was easy, for snow conditions were excellent for tracking although they hampered our own progress. The prints led us to the next lake—Tau Jhum—about a mile up-valley, often choosing a better path than ourselves, particularly so as I was anxious that none of us, including the coolies, should tread on them and obliterate the

evidence. It was mid-afternoon and our party, in varying degrees of tiredness, was now stretched out over nearly two
miles of country. The weather was obviously changing. The
mist had cleared, the sky was leaden and a bitterly chill wind
was blowing from over the mountain peaks to the northwest.
To economize our strength, most of us had now left the difficult path along the rocky foreshore and were walking on the
frozen waters of the Tau Jhum Lake. At the far end of the
lake rugged cliffs, capped with snow-fields like sugar-icing,
rose sheer. We would suddenly see wind sweep spume-like
clouds of ice particles from the snow-fields. In a few moments
the shrieking wind would hurl the spume at us from across
the lake and would literally double us up in our tracks, the ice
particles lashing our faces as if a sand-blaster had been
turned upon us. From Tau Jhum there was still two miles of
rocky country to cross before at last we reached Dudh Pokhari. By this time I was sitting down to rest every two hundred yards while Gerald, escorted by Ang Tschering and
Danu, was still an hour behind.

There is a small cluster of stone yak-herds' huts beside the
Milk Lake and from a distance I could see the Sherpa advance guard making themselves at home. The Yeti tracks
were still quite clear and here the creature had gone onto the
ice and followed closely along the shore line. I finally came to
rest on a rock about a hundred yards from the huts and it
was a good half hour before I could summon the energy to
go further. While I was sitting there I noticed that just beside the huts there was a clear sheet of water where more
duck were swimming. I then saw, with amusement, that the
Yeti had made a tentative assay across the ice towards the
water, possibly to poach a roosting duck, but had thought
better of it at the point where the ice thinned and short of
the target, had ignominiously returned supperless. Through
my glasses I saw that the Yeti had originally approached the
lake from the northwest. Neither Gerald—who was now in

sight moving slowly—nor I, had the strength to go further. Norbu had now forced the door of a small hut which conveniently proved to be three-quarters full of dry yak-dung fuel piled as high as the roof. At the far end there was just enough room for our two mattresses with the hearth between them. Two further huts provided shelter for Sherpanis and Sherpas, with a small compartment not much bigger than a dog kennel for Narayan.

That night I wrote in my diary, 'Neither of us ever expected success like this. Gerald and I *may* be the first of us to see a Yeti.'

By next morning reaction to our efforts of the day before had set in and neither Gerald nor I, in spite of the exciting stage the pursuit had reached, felt capable of walking more than a few hundred yards. I did, however, tell Ang Tschering to comb the surrounding area and collect all the evidence he could. He, Ang Tilay, Danu and Norbu, then set off in different directions.

After an early lunch I felt sufficiently recovered to climb to the top of the foothills which screened us from the Dudh Kosi glacier. As soon as I reached the edge of the glacier a stupendous sight opened up; the glacier stretched before me right up to the lateral range which forms the Tibetan frontier, Gyachung Kang being to the right and Cho Oyo to the left. The range is buttressed by towering cliffs, some of them jagged black rock, through gaps in which tremendous icefalls pour down to the head of the glacier. The glacier itself I can only describe as the world's largest rubbish heap. It is a vast area covered with immense mounds of shattered rock separated by craters whose walls are of sheer ice. The air was constantly filled with the noise of rattling stones and the crash of ice-blocks as they broke away under pressure and fell into the craters. The actual rim of the glacier was a cliff about eighty feet high, large sections of which would suddenly collapse in clouds of dust as they were undermined from below.

LEFT: A line of Yeti footprints (*Royal Geographical Society and Alpine Club of Great Britain*)
BELOW: A Yeti footprint measured against an ice ax (*Royal Geographical Society and Alpine Club of Great Britain*)

LEFT: Sir Edmund Hillary in full climbing outfit *(P. A Reuter)*
BELOW: Makalu, with Kanchenjunga in the distance on the left *(Royal Geographical Society and Alpine Club of Great Britain)*

The glacier was a fascinating sight and I watched it for over an hour until I became chilled by the cutting wind. Making a detour on the way home I suddenly came across some enormous footprints where some creature had stepped off the rocks and onto the snow. The tracks were fresh, in fact could scarcely have been more than an hour or so old. If the footprints had been made by a Yeti it was truly an enormous one; far bigger than my previous conceptions of it. I confess I was very frightened. I followed the prints for a short distance as they wove in and out of the foothills beside the edge of the glacier until my courage failed me and, pausing only for some photographs, I turned back to camp for reinforcements. It was after taking a short cut that the bitter truth dawned on me. I again came on the tracks but this time the briefest scrutiny revealed the fact that they had come directly from the camp. It was not long before I learned amid uproarious laughter from the Sherpas that their author was none other than Ang Tschering himself!

We turned in early that night and the following morning Gerald set out with Danu to take up an observation post in the foothills which I had visited the day before. I therefore set off, this time accompanied by Ang Tschering, to explore the ablation valley which leads from the lake northwards beside the glacier.

The snow lay very thick and, continually stumbling into drifts, we made very slow progress. But to our astonishment we soon came upon the tracks of a third Yeti. This one had quite clearly come down the ablation valley from the north. His home was therefore separated by a 19,000-foot range from that of Yeti No. 2 who had arrived at the lake from the northwest. It was easy to see from the tracks of Yeti No. 3 it had been more timid than No. 2. Instead of taking to the ice, No. 3 had approached the lake through the foothills, giving the few stone huts on the shore a wide berth. Yeti No. 3's tracks were approximately the same age as those of No. 2. Ang Tschering and I followed No. 3 northwards to a height which must have been near 18,000 feet which, owing to the difficult snow conditions, was all that I could manage if I was to get back to the camp without collapsing. Along the trail we found ample evidence that a Yeti, being a biped, has exactly the same troubles in crossing crusted or wind-slab snow as do human beings. Whereas an animal such as a wolf, distributing its weight equally on its four feet, could run lightly over the crust, the Yeti found that sometimes the crust would bear its weight—in which case it left little or no trace—and sometimes it would not, whereupon it left whole lengths of great plunging footsteps. Yeti No. 3 had placed itself in one situation which I found particularly interesting. It had been scrambling over rocks or boulder-hopping when it suddenly became confronted with a deep, steeply rising snow-drift. There was no easy detour and the Yeti had finally jumped into the middle of the drift, threshing, floundering and "swimming" its way upwards, using its arms and legs. The result was a great depression in the snow roughly the shape of a broad arrowhead. This suggests that the Yeti is capable of simultaneous lateral movements of its arms as in the breast stroke and I can think of no other animal likely to be found at such altitudes which would be capable of such movements.

The light was failing when Ang Tschering and I abandoned the trail at a point where the creature had climbed up the cliff from the glacier.

When we got back to camp I was more exhausted than I had ever been before during the whole trip. Gerald was in scarcely better shape, for he had remained far too long in his hide-out, exposed to the chill winds. We had reached such a limit of fatigue that neither of us had the energy to sympathise with the other. We did, however, decide that after making a brief search together along the track of Yeti No. 2 to satisfy ourselves that it had gone beyond our reach, we would push after Yeti No. 3 and establish another advance camp further up the valley to the north.

These plans were interrupted the next morning by the arrival of a runner from Katmandu. The advent of the mail-bag was the most pleasurable event of the month but on this occasion it meant discontinuing further operations for at least two days. I now had a mass of material from which to write a story and both of us had received a large number of important letters which had to be dealt with before we could release the runner for his homeward journey. The weather in the afternoon, however, proved far too good to waste and we therefore decided to dispose of Yeti No. 2. This time Gerald and I went off together accompanied by Ang Tschering, Danu and Narayan. We climbed along the side of the mountain to the north of the lake, making a long slanting traverse which finally brought us to the upland depression. From here, looking east, we had a glorious view of the summit of Everest, its snow plume boiling away like a tea kettle. But regarding Yeti No. 2 we could only confirm Danu's previous assertion that it was untraceable once it had reached a series of rock ledges on the northern side of the depression. One thing was quite certain, that it could not have come down from the north where the cliffs were unclimbable. It was possible that its hide-out could be nearby, but more probable that it had found its way over from the Bhote Kosi. If this was so it was well beyond the scope of a single afternoon's excursion.

Back at the hut we spent a pleasant evening re-reading our letters and a bundle of newspapers and enjoying an unexpected windfall in the shape of an extra bottle of rum which had come up with the mail from Katmandu.

The whole of Sunday, March 7th, was spent in writing dispatches, making out film logs and dealing with the remainder of our mail. Early the next morning our runner was handed the mail-bag and set off for Katmandu. The weather, which had improved in the past two days, now showed rather unpleasant signs of changing again. There was a turbulence of cloud at the head of the valley where two winds from different quarters appeared to be meeting. Although we were compelled to keep a wary eye on our food stock we decided to push on to the north and establish a light camp beside Lake Tanak, the next lake above us. For this excursion we took with us Ang Tschering, Ang Tilay, Danu and Norbu and seven coolies who were to carry up the loads and then return to the Dudh Pokhari camp. The snow had melted to a great extent and the going was far easier than when Ang Tschering and I had followed the same route three days before. The tracks of Yeti No. 3 were still quite visible although considerably enlarged by melting. The high altitude—the highest Gerald had ever experienced—affected us both and we did not arrive at Lake Tanak until two-thirty in the afternoon. Here, as at the Dudh Pokhari, a line of foothills separates the glacier from the waters of the lake. When we topped the last rise and looked down at the scene we were astonished to see that the snow which covered the ground literally abounded with Yeti tracks. It seemed impossible that one animal could make so many and we were forced to the conclusion that there must be a Yeti No. 4. There was, however, very little time left that afternoon for further investigation. The weather was now definitely worsening and once more thick cloud-banks were creeping up the valley from the south. I therefore ordered the coolies to dump their loads, which included a large quantity of firewood, for there was no longer any local fuel to be had, and return to the Dudh Pokhari without delay. We had two tents with us, Gerald's 'Hilary,' which we gave to the four Sherpas, and my Pyramid which Gerald and I shared. It had now turned bitterly cold and snow was falling gently. As we did not wish to waste our firewood we climbed into our sleeping-bags at four in the afternoon and ate our dinner in bed. The next morning Ang Tschering and I set off northwards continuing up the ablation valley, where the snow was now very thick. We were still tracking Yeti No. 3

although the trail was quite obliterated in places over distances of a hundred yards or so. We had just come in sight of
the next lake—Lake Masumba—when we started to sink up to
our thighs in the snow. At Ang Tschering's suggestion we
therefore climbed eastwards onto the lateral moraine of the
glacier, where we found the going easier along the exact edge
of the cliff rising from the glacier proper, although it was
more than disconcerting suddenly to hear whole sections of
the cliff disappear in a roar of rocks and clouds of dust, sometimes behind and sometimes in front of us.

The further north we advanced the more the country to
the east began to unfold for we had passed the range of
mountains which form the head of the Chola Khola valley.
Opposite Lake Masumba, which we reached at about eleven
o'clock, we were rewarded by a most magnificent view of
Everest. Indeed from no other vantage-point have I ever seen
so much of the mountain revealed. Beyond Masumba the
rocks were very loose beneath the snow and we had not advanced very far in the direction of Lake Kyja Sumba before
snow began to fall again. This decided us to turn for home.
I had been going far better than usual and on return I found
that Gerald had also been going well. He had found a good
hide-out on the mountain-side above Tanak and had once
even thought that he had seen a Yeti. Glasses had revealed,
however, that this particular Yeti was Sherpa Norbu.

Norbu now introduced an innovation into our routine by
producing a large bag of Yeti droppings which he had gathered from around the lake. Near the tent Gerald had been
excited to find a place where a Yeti had leaped thrice to extri-
cate itself from a snow-drift. Together we went back to the
tracks and took photographs of the marks in the snow. That
was the last night we were to spend in Tanak.

Next day we woke to find snow lying heavily on the tent
and further snow still falling steadily. As the fuel at Tanak
was too scanty to risk being snowed in there was nothing to

do but to retreat to the Dudh Pokhari. It was as well we did so for snow fell incessantly for the next two days. We were now properly snowbound in our Dudh Pokhari yak-hut. Further search was not only impossible in the conditions, it was useless, for all previous traces of tracks were now buried by a thick blanket of fresh snow. It was as if the Yeti had been presented with a clean sheet of paper upon which to sketch out his new movements. Unless he did so there was no longer any hope of keeping in touch with him.

On March 11th snow was still falling, but no longer as heavily as before. Ang Tschering, Norbu, Danu and Narayan were out soon after breakfast looking for tracks but without success. Gerald and I were held back in the camp by the most welcome arrival of a messenger from Tom Stobart. It appeared that the runner we had sent off to Katmandu had told some story of our finding Yeti tracks at the Base Camp as he passed through. This news had been relayed to Tom in the Chola Khola valley. Tom wrote:

Dear Ralph,
We have heard that you have seen tracks so your news may by now be more exciting than ours—however, I think you ought to have a report from us. We are camped at Thula, between Phalong Karpa and Lobuje. On the way up we had no special experience except to examine again the scalp at Pangbuche. Personally I would not rule out its being a 'mode article.' When one considers the shrunken heads made in South America it is by no means impossible. I should think a boar would provide the basic materials.

At our base. John made a recce with Doc. Edgar up the Chola Khola and visited a col with views of Everest. He saw *bear prints* and other usual animals but nothing of special note. What is this bear—the red bear?

Our small traps have been successful and we have caught three very attractive voles—short tails, rabbit-colour with white bellies and a wonderful fluffy pet. This animal is so tame that it can be handled as a pet mouse *immediately on capture. In fact all the small animals seem completely tame up here.*

This morning (8th) John and Doc. set out to cross the col to visit you as arranged. However tonight on the radio they report numerous Yeti prints on the glacier and so there is a change of plan.

These tracks are fresh, a day old, and there is a chance we have the Yeti trapped in the Chola Khola. I have told John to move his camp to an O.P. above the col. Tomorrow we all move up—leaving a block party in the narrow exit to the valley (just below our camp). I hope to meet John and post O.P.'s all over the valley, with radio contact—and then keep watch. The Yeti must come out to feed and drink.

I think that our policy of splitting up is a dangerous one myself. At least now we ought to join forces. Suggest you try to join us over the pass. If you could move up towards it we will send someone over as soon as this first Yeti scare is over.

Now we have a line and a definite area to block and work I am feeling more hopeful.

I also feel that Gerald would be absolutely invaluable with these traps, because they involve quite a bit of work and someone tied to the base. I have taken a lot of pictures of the 'cute woolly mice' which would amuse the children, also a picture of Chunk trying to get a 'mouse' out of Stan's clothes after it had run up his sleeve; and I should imagine that a fierce Tibetan wolf on a stick-lead would make a worthwhile picture to keep the ball rolling—if we can get one. Hope you and Gerald are enjoying yourselves.

Yours,
Tom.

In view of Tom's news and also in view of the fact that there was no particular point in remaining where we were now that we were out of touch with the Yeti, we decided to retreat down the valley to Ang Tilay's house in Nah village. This journey we completed in very orderly fashion in spite of the fresh snow. This time when we arrived at Nah visibility was perfect and for the first time we saw the second valley which leads north-eastwards up the side of the glacier from its terminal moraine. With sinking hearts we realized its significance. This was the perfect second escape route by which at least two Yeti could have avoided us had they wished to get back to the north. It was also possible that somewhere up this ablation valley there was a pass over to the Chola Khola as Tom seemed to suggest. It might even be one of our own Yeti which was now engaging Tom and John's attention in the Chola Khola. That evening I drew a sketch-map of our movements and sent the following reply to Tom:

Dear Tom,

Very many thanks for your letter of the 8th, with its heartening news, which arrived yesterday. To save time I am enclosing copies of two stories sent to London and a rough sketch-map which together should tell you our story. We have been concerned with three, almost certainly, four Yeti. We first picked up the tracks, coming down valley, just above Macherma, on about the temporary snow-line. They were about four days old otherwise I should have sounded the 'Tally-ho' for you all, but did not do so in case we diverted you from more recent discoveries. It was also no good trying to track them on grass so we went on up valley, to try and track them to source. (I may say that as all were facing down valley—i.e. south—and into the sun when it was shining, it was a difficult job getting adequate pictures, particularly of such details as the distinctive toe features.) As we went upwards the snow remained good and a fascinating picture unfolded itself from the tracks. Three Yeti started simultaneously from different points of the compass and we think it must have been the heavy snowfall of the night of Feb. 26th which sent them down in search of food. In addition, a fourth Yeti has apparently been fooling about with Yeti 3, round Lake Tanak. There were no Yeti marks as high as Lake Masumba and altho' I cannot find complete proof I should bet that Nos. 3 and 4 climbed into the ablation valley from the right, about half-way between the two lakes.

I would come across to visit you but there is no pass apparent to me on this side, that is nothing that would not require some moderately expert climbing, and being a novice I think it would be foolish to lead the Sherpas into obvious trouble.

I know we all have personal likes etc., but to my mind there is no question but that this valley is the best bet yet—you will excuse us if the report of a *single* Yeti's tracks now leaves us rather cold. If your own scare dies down I would suggest a concerted effort here, a pincer movement up the two forks of the Dudh Kosi meeting at the foot of Gyachung Kang. This could cut off lateral retreat.

Our plan is to probe up the right-hand fork of the Dudh Kosi and we should be back at the Base Camp about Wednesday or Thursday (March 17/18th); our rations are two meals light of estimate as two tins of kippers vanished. Please try and meet us there to discuss plans.

If you can't make Wednesday or Thursday can you let us know? Also please let me know which particular col or pass needs watching, bearing in mind we do not have a good map here. I may be able to discover a pass in the meantime and will do my best. Both of us are very well and still fairly optimistic. Good luck and good hunting to all of you.

Yours,
Ralph

The runner carrying this message made astonishingly good time for three days later he was back again bringing a second letter from Tom. It ran:

Dear Ralph,

Indeed you seem to have had better luck than we have, because we only found the tracks of one Yeti—just possibly two—up here. At the moment we do not believe that the range between you and us is crossable by Yeti. This seems to show that the Yeti is not as rare as all that since ours is a different one. Your pace 2 ft. 3 in. exactly corresponds with my measurements, but regarding the tracks we measured both Bill Edgar and myself and John all had the impression that the animal was walking on all fours.

I am sending John and Stan and Doc. up to the other col to-day to see if they can see you. If so I shall be over. If not will see you at Base on Wednesday or Thursday.

I should like to go down to Ghat to see the flowers for a few days when we get back if this is possible. It is a bit difficult for me so far because I am somehow bound to make a film of this expedition. Unfortunately to make a film I have to get pictures. I cannot bring in wolves or reconstructions of Yeti sliding down on their behinds without getting pictures of the damned things.

However let us hope we get to grips with Yeti soon, then we shall have more time for the other things.

See you soon. All well and keen.

Tom.

The intervening days before this reply came were spent in exhausting reconnaissances. On Saturday, March 13th, I set off with Ang Tschering, Ang Tilay, and Norbu up the eastern fork of the Dudh Kosi. We began by climbing up the terminal moraine of the Dudh Kosi glacier.

Glaciers are tiring in the extreme to negotiate, for the surface towards the snout is generally composed of loose pebbles and shale, and by the time we had climbed down to the foot of the eastern ablation valley I already felt we had done a normal day's work. We came down at a point where there are three or four herdsmen's huts sheltered beneath an immense cliff of black rock. The huts are known as taknak which means 'Black Rock.' From the huts a frozen waterfall—as distinct from an ice-fall, for this one obviously melts in summer and becomes a torrent—winds very steeply upwards in the general direction of Taweche. We decided to make our way up it; to me, it seemed an interminable ascent as we climbed with the black cliff to our left over "boiler plates" of bubbly, blue ice. It must have taken us two hours to reach the top, this time with myself lagging a good quarter of a mile behind the others. At the summit the route branches; we took the right-hand fork which brought us hard up against the fluted ice-cliffs which form Taweche's main defences. Had we taken the left-hand fork which leads more to the north we should have arrived at the foot of the col which John was preparing to cross. This particular col was unknown to Ang Tilay although his home is within a few miles of it. It is possible that had we not inadvertently by-passed it we should have seen John's party bivouacked on the summit.

The route we chose led to the top of a steep ridge which disclosed a large area of rolling upland between Taweche and the Dudh Kosi river-bed. This 'pastoral shelf,' which was invisible from below, looked like ideal Yeti country to me but we never found any tracks upon it. We now turned south along the ridge, which itself was high enough to merit the Sherpas building a cairn upon it. Most of the flank of the Taweche range was exposed, but seen from close range none of the gaps in it look climbable even by a fully equipped party of experts. A secondary feature to the north hid John's col from view. A long downhill scramble to the south brought us by a roundabout route to a point opposite Nah, which lay possibly two thousand feet below. The descent was not difficult but now even the Sherpas were tiring. I was so exhausted that I could scarcely manage the stepping-stones across the river and nearly foundered on the steep short climb up to Ang Tilay's house. Throughout the day the sun had shone brilliantly and I was suffering badly from glacier burn.

Next day we returned to the western fork of the Dudh Kosi to examine the vast amphitheatre of boulders and shattered rock which we had noted had been visited by the first two Yeti which we had contacted on our journey upwards. We felt that we owed this to Major de la Bastide, for a close study of our map showed us that this was the exact spot which the Major had indicated to us by radiethesia as a Yeti haunt. Gerald, having produced this particular 'secret weapon,' was perfectly confident that the Major would be correct in his diagnosis, although I remained sceptical. We climbed up the amphitheatre, which we named affectionately the 'Frenchman's Gully,' until, at about 18,000 feet under an overhang which had been sheltered from the recent snowfall, we once more came on Yeti tracks which were possibly ten days old. Beside the tracks were more droppings identical with those we had previously analyzed. At this height Gerald and I decided we could go no farther, but the three Sherpas with us climbed on for another eight hundred feet without discovering any further evidence. By the middle of the afternoon we had between us covered every inch of the gully and were satisfied that there were no longer any Yetis within it, but, as Gerald was again at pains to point out, Major de la Bastide could not predict the future with his pendulum; he could only tell where the creature was at the moment he was making his experiments.

Throughout the day the sun had again been fierce and by the evening when we returned to Ang Tilay's house my face was very badly burnt indeed. In spite of anti-glacier burn creams—learnt later that I was probably allergic to the first one I used—the irritation was so maddening that I spent an entirely sleepless night. It was this that decided us to move the camp back to Macherma for it was obvious that I should not be able to continue working among the high altitude snows for some time and our food was now running short. On the valley floor the snows had vanished quickly under the sun of the two previous days and what had seemed quite a lengthy march as we had come up-river, hampered additionally as we had been by fog, proved a short easy march going down. We reached Macherma in mid-morning. In the small lateral valley at Macherma there was far less snow than when Charles and I had tried to climb the cliff at its head. As my face was still very painful I decided to spend the rest of the day in the hut, but Ang Tschering, Ang Tilay, Norbu and Danu, spurred on by the fact that I had offered a fresh reward now that most previous tracks had been obliterated, were anxious to try the cliff. According to Ang Tilay, there was another shelf above the cliffs which led to a small plateau used for summer grazing and upon which stood a few deserted huts known as Lang Soma. The four Sherpas then set off to climb the gully to the north of the cliff which had previously defeated Gerald and myself and after making a remarkable high altitude detour round to the south returned to the camp at about 5 p.m. They claimed to have found six-day-old tracks of a 'small Yeti' but were the first to admit that this did not merit a reward.

Going over the food stocks the next morning we were forced to the conclusion that we no longer had enough supplies to make another useful sortie. We therefore decided to return to Base Camp. When we reached Dolle this time the yak-herd who had reported tracks to Gerald as he was returning from our first sortie was present in his hut. He confirmed what he had previously reported; that he had found tracks high up a small lateral valley at Dolle and he escorted me for a short distance up the valley to point out the place. Again it was what we had come to recognize as 'good Yeti country.' We had just returned to Dolle when a Sherpa runner approached us coming down-valley. He brought the news that Tom Stobart, John and Bill Edgar had crossed into the Dudh Kosi valley and spent the night at Char Chung high up above Nah under Taweche peak. A brief note from Tom said that John and Bill Edgar were returning over the col they had crossed while Tom himself would follow us down to the Base Camp. Tom actually caught us up just below Phorche, where Gerald and I had stopped for tea before pushing on for home. We spent many hours that night talking round the camp-fire recounting our adventures of the past few days and discussing future plans. . . .

Next morning I had just completed a bath and dressed in clean clothes when an agitated Sherpa yak-herd named Arjeab arrived from Macherma to say that the previous night he had heard the Yeti call repeatedly close to the huts there. On being asked what the call was like he strode up and down the camp imitating a strange mewing sound which again resembled the amplified crying of a sea gull. It may seem strange that we did not set off at once back to Macherma. The truth is that none of us had the energy to do so. Herein lies the crux of sorties at high altitude. It is impossible to

sustain effort indefinitely and certainly in my case nearly
three weeks of strenuous work was all I could ever manage
without some days' rest. That Arjeab seriously believed he
had heard a Yeti I have no doubt. On leaving the camp he
went straight to Thyangboche Monastery to undergo a
'cleansing ceremony' to ward off any evil that might befall
him after hearing the call. He would scarcely have taken this
trouble if he had been merely yarn-spinning.

SIR EDMUND HILLARY

HIGH ADVENTURE

(From HIGH ADVENTURE. New York: E. P. Dutton & Co., Inc., 1955)

We had climbed to Camp Nine, and were waiting to make the final assault on Everest. George Lowe, Alf Gregory and Ang Nyima, a Sherpa porter, the three who formed our last assault party, left us, and we went on alone.

I watched our support party disappear down the ridge and then turned to examine our camp site more closely. It wasn't really much of a place. Above us was a rock cliff—black and craggy, but at least devoid of loose stones to fall on us. From the foot of the cliff a little snow slope ran at an easy angle for eight or nine feet to the top of the steep and exposed south face of the mountain. This little slope was to be our camp site. It was certainly far from flat and it was going to need a lot of work on it before we could possibly pitch a tent. We carefully moved all the gear to one side and then set to work with our ice axes to remove the surface snow off a reasonably large area. Ten inches down, we struck rock and after half an hour's hard work we had cleared an area about eight feet long and six feet wide. The slope underneath was made up of stones and rubble all firmly glued together with ice. This was much harder going. With the picks on our ice axes we chopped away at the slope, prizing out the separate stones and scraping away the rubble. But our progress was very slow. We weren't using any oxygen at all, but we found we could work very hard indeed for periods of ten minutes or

43

so. Then we'd have to stop and have a short rest. With the debris we chopped out of the slope we tried to build up the platform on the downhill side, but almost invariably saw it collapse and go roaring down over the bluffs below. At times we were buffeted by wind and snow, yet we worked doggedly on, knowing that our tent was our only chance of survival against the rigors of the night.

At 6:30 A.M. we crawled slowly out of the tent and stood on our little ledge. Already the upper part of the mountain was bathed in sunlight. It looked warm and inviting, but our ledge was dark and cold. We lifted our oxygen onto our backs and slowly connected up the tubes to our face masks. My thirty-pound load seemed to crush me downward and stifled all enthusiasm, but when I turned on the oxygen and breathed it deeply, the burden seemed to lighten and the old urge to get to grips with the mountain came back. We strapped on our crampons and tied on our nylon rope; grasped our ice axes and were ready to go.

I looked at the way ahead. From our tent very steep slopes covered with deep powder snow led up to a prominent snow shoulder on the southeast ridge about a hundred feet above our heads. The slopes were in the shade and breaking trail was going to be cold work. Still a little worried about my boots, I asked Tenzing to lead off. Always willing to do his share, and more than his share if necessary, Tenzing scrambled past me and tackled the slope. With powerful thrusts of his legs he forced his way up in knee-deep snow. I gathered in the rope and followed along behind him.

We were climbing out over the tremendous south face of the mountain and below us snow chutes and rock ribs plummeted thousands of feet down to the Western Cwm. Starting in the morning straight on to exposed climbing is always trying on the nerves and this was no exception. In imagination I could feel my heavy load dragging me back-

ward down the great slopes below; I seemed clumsy and unstable and my breath was hurried and uneven. But Tenzing
was pursuing an irresistible course up the slope and I didn't
have time to think too much. My muscles soon warmed up
to their work, my nerves relaxed, and I dropped into the old
climbing rhythm and followed steadily up his tracks. As we
gained a little height we moved into the rays of the sun and
although we could feel no appreciable warmth, we were
greatly encouraged by its presence. Taking no rests, Tenzing
plowed his way up through the deep snow and led out onto
the snow shoulder. We were now at a height of 28,000 feet.
Towering directly above our heads was the south summit—
steep and formidable. And to the right were the enormous
cornices of the summit ridge. We still had a long way to go.

Ahead of us the ridge was sharp and narrow but rose at
an easy angle. I felt warm and strong now, so took over the
lead. First I investigated the ridge with my ice ax. On the
sharp crest of the ridge and on the right-hand side loose
powder snow was lying dangerously over hard ice. Any attempt to climb on this would only produce an unpleasant
slide down toward the Kangshung glacier. But the left-hand
slope was better—it was still rather steep, but it had a firm
surface of wind-blown powder snow into which our crampons
would bite readily.

Taking every care, I moved along onto the left-hand side
of the ridge. Everything seemed perfectly safe. With increased confidence I took another step. Next moment I was
almost thrown off-balance as the wind crust suddenly gave
way and I sank through it up to my knee. It took me a little
while to regain my breath. Then I gradually pulled my leg
out of the hole. I was almost upright again when the wind
crust under the other foot gave way and I sank back with
both legs enveloped in soft loose snow to the knees. It was
the mountaineer's curse—breakable crust. I forced my way
along. Sometimes for a few careful steps I was on the surface,

but usually the crust would break at the critical moment and I'd be up to my knees again. Though it was tiring and exasperating work, I felt I had plenty of strength in reserve. For half an hour I continued on in this uncomfortable fashion, with the violent balancing movements I was having to make completely destroying rhythm and breath. It was a great relief when the snow condition improved and I was able to stay on the surface. I still kept down on the steep slopes on the left of the ridge, but plunged ahead and climbed steadily upward. I came over a small crest and saw in front of me a tiny hollow on the ridge. And in this hollow lay two oxygen bottles almost completely covered with snow. It was Evans's and Bourdillon's dump.

I rushed forward into the hollow and knelt beside them. Wrenching one of the bottles out of its frozen bed I wiped the snow off its dial—it showed a thousand pounds pressure —it was nearly a third full of oxygen. I checked the other—it was the same. This was great news. It meant that the oxygen we were carrying on our backs only had to get us back to these bottles instead of right down to the South Col. It gave us more than another hour of endurance. I explained this to Tenzing through my oxygen mask. I don't think he understood, but he realized I was pleased about something and nodded enthusiastically.

I led off again. I knew there was plenty of hard work ahead and Tenzing could save his energies for that. The ridge climbed on upward rather more steeply now and then broadened out and shot up at a sharp angle to the foot of the enormous slope running up to the south summit. I crossed over onto the right-hand side of the ridge and found the snow was firm there. I started chipping a long line of steps up to the foot of the great slope. Here we stamped out a platform for ourselves and I checked our oxygen. Everything seemed to be going well. I had a little more oxygen left than Tenzing, which meant I was obtaining a slightly lower flow rate from

my set, but it wasn't enough to matter and there was nothing
I could do about it anyway.

Ahead of us was a really formidable problem and I stood
in my steps and looked at it. Rising from our feet was an
enormous slope slanting steeply down onto the precipitous
east face of Everest and climbing up with appalling steepness
to the south summit of the mountain four hundred feet above
us. The left-hand side of the slope was a most unsavory mix-
ture of steep loose rock and snow, which my New Zealand
training immediately regarded with grave suspicion, but
which in actual fact the rock-climbing Britons, Evans and
Bourdillon, had ascended in much trepidation when on the
first assault. The only other route was up the snow itself and
still fairly discernible here and there were traces of the track
made by the first assault party, who had come down it in
preference to their line of ascent up the rocks. The snow
route it was for us! There looked to be some tough work
ahead and as Tenzing had been taking it easy for a while I
hardheartedly waved him through. With his first six steps I
realized that the work was going to be much harder than I
had thought. His first two steps were on top of the snow, the
third was up to his ankles, and by the sixth he was up to his
hips. But almost lying against the steep slope, he drove himself onward, plowing a track directly upward. Even following in his steps was hard work, for the loose snow refused to
pack into safe steps. After a long and valiant spell he was
plainly in need of a rest, so I took over.

Immediately I realized that we were on dangerous ground.
On this very steep slope the snow was soft and deep with
little coherence. My ice ax shaft sank into it without any support and we had no form of a belay. The only factor that
made it at all possible to progress was a thin crust of frozen
snow which tied the whole slope together. But this crust was
a poor support. I was forcing my way upward, plunging deep
steps through it, when suddenly with a dull breaking noise

an area of crust all around me about six feet in diameter broke off into large sections and slid with me back through three or four steps. And then I stopped; but the crust gathering speed, slithered on out of sight. It was a nasty shock. My whole training told me that the slope was exceedingly dangerous, but at the same time I was saying to myself, "Ed, my boy, this is Everest—you've got to push it a bit harder!" My solar plexus was tight with fear as I plowed on. Halfway up I stopped, exhausted. I could look down ten thousand feet between my legs and I have never felt more insecure. Anxiously I waved Tenzing up to me.

"What do you think of it, Tenzing?" And the immediate response, "Very bad, very dangerous!" "Do you think we should go on?" and there came the familiar reply that never helped you much but never let you down: "Just as you wish!" I waved him on to take a turn at leading. Changing the lead much more frequently now, we made our unhappy way upward, sometimes sliding back and wiping out half a dozen steps and never feeling confident that at any moment the whole slope might not avalanche. In the hope of some sort of a belay we traversed a little toward the rocks but found no help in their smooth holdless surface. We plunged on upward. And then I noticed that, a little above us, the left-hand rock ridge turned into snow and the snow looked firm and safe. Laboriously and carefully we climbed across some steep rock and I sank my ice ax shaft into the snow of the ridge. It went in firm and hard. The pleasure of this safe belay after all the uncertainty below was like a reprieve to a condemned man. Strength flowed into my limbs and I could feel my tense nerves and muscles relaxing. I swung my ice ax at the slope and started chipping a line of steps upward— it was very steep but seemed so gloriously safe. Tenzing, an inexpert but enthusiastic step-cutter, took a turn and chopped a haphazard line of steps up another pitch. We were making fast time now and the slope was starting to ease off. Tenzing gallantly waved me through and with a growing feeling of excitement I cramponed up some firm slopes to the rounded top of the south summit. It was only 9 A.M.

With intense interest I looked at the vital ridge leading to the summit—the ridge about which Evans and Bourdillon had made such gloomy forecasts. At first glance it was an exceedingly impressive and indeed a frightening sight. In the narrow crest of this ridge, the basic rock of the mountain had a thin capping of snow and ice—ice that reached out over the east face in enormous cornices, overhanging and treacherous, and only waiting for the careless foot of the mountaineer to break off and crash ten thousand feet to the Kangshung glacier. And from the cornices the snow dropped steeply to the left to merge with the enormous rock bluffs which towered eight thousand feet above the Western Cwm. It was impressive all right! But as I looked my fears started to lift a little. Surely I could see a route there? For this snow slope on the left, although very steep and exposed, was practically continuous for the first half of the ridge, although in places the great cornices reached hungrily across. If we could make a route along that snow slope we could go quite a distance at least.

With a feeling almost of relief I set to work with my ice ax and cut a platform for myself just down off the top of the south summit. Tenzing did the same and then we removed our oxygen sets and sat down. The day was still remarkably fine and we felt no discomfort through our thick layers of clothing from either wind or cold. We had a drink out of Tenzing's water bottle and then I checked our oxygen supplies. Tenzing's bottle was practically exhausted but mine still had a little in it. As well as this we each had a full bottle. I decided that the difficulties ahead would demand as light a weight on our backs as possible so determined to use only the full bottles. I removed Tenzing's empty bottle and my nearly empty one and laid them in the snow. With particular care I connected up our last bottles and tested to see that they were working efficiently. The needles on the dials were steady on 3,300 pounds per square inch pressure—they were very full bottles holding just over 800 liters of oxygen each. At 3 liters a minute we consumed 180 liters an hour and this meant a total endurance of nearly 4½ hours. This didn't seem much for the problems ahead, but I was determined if necessary to cut down to 2 liters a minute for the homeward trip.

I was greatly encouraged to find how, even at 28,700 feet and with no oxygen, I could work out slowly but clearly the problems of mental arithmetic that the oxygen supply demanded. A correct answer was imperative—any mistake could well mean a trip with no return. But we had no time to waste. I stood up and took a series of photographs in every direction then thrust my camera back to its warm home inside my clothing. I heaved my now pleasantly light oxygen load onto my back and connected up my tubes. I did the same for Tenzing and we were ready to go. I asked Tenzing to belay me and then with a growing air of excitement I cut a broad and safe line of steps down to the snow saddle below the south summit. I wanted an easy route when we came back up here weak and tired. Tenzing came down the steps and joined me and then belayed once again.

I moved along onto the steep snow slope on the left side of the ridge. With the first blow of my ice ax my excitement increased. The snow—to my astonishment—was crystalline and hard. A couple of rhythmical blows of the ice ax produced a step that was big enough even for our oversize high-altitude boots. But best of all the steps were strong and safe. A little conscious of the great drops beneath me, I chipped a line of steps for the full length of the rope—forty feet—and then forced the shaft of my ice ax firmly into the snow. It made a fine belay and I looped the rope around it. I waved to Tenzing to join me and as he moved slowly and carefully along the steps I took in the rope as I went on cutting steps. It was exhilarating work—the summit ridge of Everest, the crisp snow and the smooth easy blows of the ice ax all combined to make me feel a greater sense of power than I had ever felt at great altitudes before. I went on cutting for rope length after rope length.

We were now approaching a point where one of the great cornices was encroaching onto our slope. We'd have to go down to the rocks to avoid it. I cut a line of steps steeply down the slope to a small ledge on top of the rocks. There wasn't much room, but it made a reasonably safe stance. I waved to Tenzing to join me. As he came down to me I realized there was something wrong with him. I had been so absorbed in the technical problems of the ridge that I hadn't thought much about Tenzing except for a vague feeling that he seemed to move along the steps with unnecessary slowness. But now it was quite obvious that he was not only moving extremely slowly but he was breathing quickly and with difficulty and was in considerable distress. I immediately suspected his oxygen set and helped him down on to the ledge so that I could examine it. The first thing I noticed was that from the outlet of his face mask there were hanging some long icicles. I looked at it more closely and found that the outlet tube—about two inches in diameter—was almost completely blocked up with ice. This was preventing Tenzing from exhaling freely and must have made it extremely unpleasant for him. Fortunately the outlet tube was made of rubber and by manipulating this with my hand I was able to release all the ice and let it fall out. The valves started operating and Tenzing was given immediate relief. Just as a check I examined my own set and found that it too had partly frozen up in the outlet tube, but not sufficiently to have affected me a great deal. I removed the ice out of it without a great deal of trouble. Automatically I looked at our pressure gauges—just over 2,900 pounds (2,900 pounds was just over 700 liters; 180 into 700 was about 4)—we had nearly four hours' endurance left. That meant we weren't going badly.

I looked at the route ahead. This next piece wasn't going to be easy. Our rock ledge was perched right on top of the enormous bluff running down into the Western Cwm. In fact, almost under my feet, I could see the dirty patch on the floor of the Cwm which I knew was Camp IV. In a sudden urge to escape our isolation I waved and shouted, and then as suddenly stopped as I realized my foolishness. Against the vast expanse of Everest, eight thousand feet above them, we'd be quite invisible to the best binoculars. I turned back to the problem ahead. The rock was far too steep to attempt to drop down and go around this pitch. The only thing to do was to try and shuffle along the ledge and cut handholds in the bulging ice that was trying to push me off it. Held on a tight rope by Tenzing, I cut a few handholds and then thrust my ice ax as hard as I could into the solid snow and ice. Using this to take my weight I moved quickly along the ledge. It proved easier than I had anticipated. A few more handholds, another quick swing across them, and I was able to cut a line of steps up onto a safe slope and chop out a roomy terrace from which to belay Tenzing as he climbed up to me.

We were now fast approaching the most formidable obstacle on the ridge—a great rock step. This step had always been visible in aerial photographs and in 1951 on the Everest Reconnaissance we had seen it quite clearly with glasses from Thyangboche. We had always thought of it as the obstacle on the ridge which could well spell defeat. I cut a line of steps across the last snow slope and then commenced traversing over a steep rock slab that led to the foot of the great step. The holds were small and hard to see and I brushed my snow glasses away from my eyes. Immediately I was blinded by a bitter wind sweeping across the ridge and laden with particles of ice. I hastily replaced my glasses and blinked away the ice and tears until I could see again. But it made me realize how efficient was our clothing in protecting us from the rigors of even a fine day at 29,000 feet. Still half blinded, I climbed across the slab and then dropped down into a tiny snow hollow at the foot of the step. And here Tenzing slowly joined me.

I looked anxiously up at the rocks. Planted squarely across the ridge in a vertical bluff, they looked extremely difficult, and I knew that our strength and ability to climb steep rock at this altitude would be severely limited. I examined the route out to the left. By dropping fifty or a hundred feet over steep slabs, we might be able to get around the bottom of the bluff, but there was no indication that we'd be able to climb back onto the ridge again. And to lose any height now might be fatal. Search as I could, I was unable to see an easy route up to the step or in fact any route at all. Finally, in desperation, I examined the right-hand end of the bluff. Attached to this and overhanging the precipitous east face was a large cornice. This cornice, in preparation for its inevitable crash down the mountainside, had started to lose its grip on the rock and a long narrow vertical crack had been formed between the rock and the ice. The crack was large enough to take the human frame and though it offered little security it was at least a route. I quickly made up my mind—Tenzing had an excellent belay and we must be near the top—it was worth a try.

Before attempting the pitch I produced my camera once again. I had no confidence that I would be able to climb this crack and with a surge of competitive pride which unfortunately afflicts even mountaineers I determined to have proof that at least we had reached a good deal higher than the south summit. I took a few photographs and then made another rapid check of the oxygen—2,550 pounds pressure.

(2,550 from 3,300 leaves 750. 750 over 3,300 is about ⅔ths. ⅔ths off 800 liters leaves about 600 liters. 600 divided by 180 is nearly 3½). Three and a half hours to go. I examined Tenzing's belay to make sure it was a good one and then slowly crawled inside the crack.

In front of me was the rock wall, vertical but with a few promising holds. Behind me was the ice wall of the cornice, glittering and hard but cracked here and there. I took a hold on the rock in front and then jammed one of my crampons hard into the ice behind. Leaning back with my oxygen set on the ice I slowly levered myself upward. Searching feverishly with my spare boot, I found a tiny ledge on the rock and took some of the weight off my other leg. Leaning back on the cornice I fought to regain my breath. Constantly at the back of my mind was the fear that the cornice might break off and my nerves were taut with suspense. But slowly I forced my way up—wriggling and jamming and using every little hold. In one place I managed to force my ice ax into a crack in the ice and this gave me the necessary purchase to get over a holdless stretch. And then I found a solid foothold in a hollow in the ice and next moment I was reaching over the top of the rock and pulling myself to safety. The rope came tight—its forty feet had been barely enough.

I lay on the little rock ledge panting furiously. Gradually it dawned on me that I was up the step and I felt a glow of pride and determination that completely subdued my temporary feelings of weakness. For the first time on the whole expedition I really knew I was going to get to the top. "It will have to be pretty tough to stop us now" was my thought. But I couldn't entirely ignore the feeling of astonishment and wonder that I'd been able to get up such a difficulty at 29,000 feet even with oxygen.

When I was breathing more evenly I stood up and, leaning over the edge, waved to Tenzing to come up. He moved into the crack and I gathered in the rope and took some of his weight. Then he, in turn, commenced to struggle and jam and force his way up until I was able to pull him to safety—gasping for breath. We rested for a moment. Above us the ridge continued on as before—enormous overhanging cornices on the right and steep snow slopes on the left running down to the rock bluffs. But the angle of the snow slopes was easing off. I went on chipping a line of steps, but thought it safe enough for us to move together in order to save time. The ridge rose up in a great series of snakelike undulations which bore away to the right, each one concealing the next. I had no idea where the top was. I'd cut a line of steps around the side of one undulation and another would come into view. We were getting desperately tired now and Tenzing was going very slowly. I'd been cutting steps for almost two hours and my back and arms were starting to tire. I tried cramponing along the slope without cutting steps, but my feet slipped uncomfortably down the slope. I went on cutting. We seemed to have been going for a very long time and my confidence was fast evaporating. Bump followed bump with maddening regularity. A patch of shingle barred our way and I climbed dully up it and started cutting steps around another bump. And then I realized that this was the last bump, for ahead of me the ridge dropped steeply away in a great corniced curve, and out in the distance I could see the pastel shades and fleecy clouds of the highlands of Tibet.

To my right a slender snow ridge climbed up to a snowy dome about forty feet above our heads. But all the way along the ridge the thought had haunted me that the summit might be the crest of a cornice. It was too late to take risks now. I asked Tenzing to belay me strongly and I started cutting a cautious line of steps up the ridge. Peering from side to side and thrusting with my ice ax I tried to discover a possible cornice, but everything seemed solid and firm. I waved Tenzing up to me. A few more whacks of the ice ax, a few very weary steps and we were on the summit of Everest.

It was 11:30 A.M. My first sensation was one of relief—relief that the long grind was over; that the summit had been reached before our oxygen supplies had dropped to a critical level; and relief that in the end the mountain had been kind to us in having a pleasantly rounded cone for its summit instead of a fearsome and unapproachable cornice. But mixed with the relief was a vague sense of astonishment that I should have been the lucky one to attain the ambition of so many brave and determined climbers. It seemed difficult at first to grasp that we'd got there. I was too tired and too conscious of the long way down to safety really to feel any great elation. But as the fact of our success thrust itself more clearly into my mind I felt a quiet glow of satisfaction spread through my body—a satisfaction less vociferous but more powerful than I had ever felt on a mountaintop before. I turned and looked at Tenzing. Even beneath his oxygen mask and the icicles hanging from his hair I could see his infectious grin of sheer delight.

CROSSING THE SUB-ANTARCTIC OCEAN IN A WHALEBOAT

(From SOUTH: THE STORY OF SHACKLETON'S LAST EXPEDITION.
London: William Heinemann Ltd., 1919)

One of the greatest of small-boat voyages was made in 1916 by the famous Antarctic explorer, Sir Ernest Shackleton, from Elephant Island to South Georgia. The Endurance, *one of the two ships of Shackleton's 1914-1917 expedition, had been beset and crushed by the ice off the Caird Coast, leaving Shackleton and twenty-seven companions to exist for five months on the drifting floes. They had little food but they did have three boats. In these, when the ice began breaking up around them, they managed to reach rocky, glacier-covered Elephant Island shortly before the Antarctic winter set in. It was then that Shackleton and five companions, in order to bring help to the rest of the party, undertook the epic boat journey described here in the leader's own words. In a battered, 22-foot whaleboat they sailed across some 800 miles of the world's stormiest ocean. After landing in South Georgia, Shackleton and two of the others crossed the island's supposedly impassable mountains and glaciers on foot. On the opposite coast they reached a whaling station, and eventually all of the Elephant Island party were rescued. The expedition's second ship, the* Aurora, *was frozen in the Ross Sea ice for almost a year before she could be extricated. This left another group of explorers stranded on the Antarctic mainland. Seven of the nine men there were also finally saved.*

A boat journey in search of relief was necessary and must not be delayed. That conclusion was forced upon me. The nearest port where assistance could certainly be secured was Port Stanley, in the Falkland Islands, 540 miles away, but we could scarcely hope to beat up against the prevailing north-westerly wind in a frail and weakened boat with a small sail area. South Georgia was over 800 miles away, but lay in the area of the west winds, and I could count upon finding whales at any of the whaling-stations on the east coast. A boat party might make the voyage and be back with relief within a month, provided that the sea was clear of ice and the boat survive the great seas. It was not difficult to decide that South Georgia must be the objective, and I proceeded to plan ways and means. The hazards of a boat journey across 800 miles of stormy, sub-Antarctic ocean were obvious, but I calculated that at worst the venture would add nothing to the risks of the men left on the island. There would be fewer mouths to feed during the winter and the boat would not require to take more than one month's provisions for six men, for if we did not make South Georgia in that time we were sure to go under. A consideration that had weight with me was that there was no chance at all of any search being made for us on Elephant Island.

The case required to be argued in some detail, since all hands knew that the perils of the proposed journey were extreme. The risk was justified solely by our urgent need of assistance. The ocean south of Cape Horn in the middle of May is known to be the most tempestuous storm-swept area of water in the world. The weather then is unsettled, the skies are dull and overcast, and the gales are almost unceasing. We had to face these conditions in a small and weather-beaten boat, already strained by the work of the months that had passed. Worsley and Wild* realized that the attempt must be made, and they both asked to be allowed to accompany me on the voyage. I told Wild at once that he would have to stay behind. I relied upon him to hold the party together while I was away and to make the best of his way to Deception Island with the men in the spring in the event of our failure to bring help. Worsley I would take with me,

* Frank Wild, the second in command.—E.H.

for I had a very high opinion of his accuracy and quickness as a navigator, and especially in the snapping and working out of positions in difficult circumstances—an opinion that was only enhanced during the actual journey. Four other men would be required, and I decided to call for volunteers. . . . I finally selected McNeish, McCarthy, and Vincent in addition to Worsley and Crean. The crew seemed a strong one, and as I looked at the men I felt confidence increasing.

The decision made, I walked through the blizzard with Worsley and Wild to examine the *James Caird*. The 20-ft. boat had never looked big; she appeared to have shrunk in some mysterious way when I viewed her in the light of our new undertaking. She was an ordinary ship's whaler, fairly strong, but showing signs of the strains she had endured since the crushing of the *Endurance*. Where she was holed in leaving the pack was, fortunately, about the water-line and easily patched. Standing beside her, we glanced at the fringe of the storm-swept, tumultuous sea, that formed our path. Clearly, our voyage would be a big adventure. I called the carpenter and asked him if he could do anything to make the boat more seaworthy. He first inquired if he was to go with me, and seemed quite pleased when I said "Yes." He was over fifty years of age and not altogether fit, but he had a good knowledge of sailing-boats and was very quick. McCarthy said that he could contrive some sort of covering for the *James Caird* if he might use the lids of the cases and the four sledge-runners that we had lashed inside the boat for use in the event of a landing on Graham Land at Wilhelmina Bay. This bay, at one time the goal of our desire, had been left behind in the course of our drift, but we had retained the runners. The carpenter proposed to complete the covering with some of our canvas, and he set about making his plans at once. . . .

Our last night on the solid ground of Elephant Island was

cold and uncomfortable. We turned out at dawn and had breakfast. Then we launched the *Stancomb Wills** and loaded her with stores, gear, and ballast, which would be transferred to the *James Caird* when the heavier boat had been launched. The ballast consisted of bags made from blankets and filled with sand, making a total weight of about 1000 lb. In addition we had gathered a number of round boulders and about 250 lb. of ice, which would supplement our two casks of water. . . .

The swell was slight when the *Stancomb Wills* was launched and the boat got under way without any difficulty; but half an hour later, when we were pulling down the *James Caird*, the swell increased suddenly. Apparently the movement of the ice outside had made an opening and allowed the sea to run in without being blanketed by the line of pack. The swell made things difficult. Many of us got wet to the waist while dragging the boat out—a serious matter in that climate. When the *James Caird* was afloat in the surf she nearly capsized among the rocks before we could get her clear, and Vincent and the carpenter, who were on the deck, were thrown into the water. This was really bad luck, for the two men would have small chance of drying their clothes after we had got under way. Hurley, who had the eye of the professional photographer for "incidents," secured a picture of the upset, and I firmly believe that he would have liked the two unfortunate men to remain in the water until he could get a "snap" at close quarters; but we hauled them out immediately, regardless of his feelings.

The *James Caird* was soon clear of the breakers. We used all the available ropes as a long painter to prevent her drifting away to the north-east, and then the *Stancomb Wills* came alongside, transferred her load, and went back to the shore for more. As she was being beached this time the sea took her stern and half filled her with water. She had to be

* Another of the expedition's boats, lighter than the *James Caird*.—E.H.

turned over and emptied before the return journey could be made. Every member of the crew of the *Stancomb Wills* was wet to the skin. The water-casks were towed behind the *Stancomb Wills* on this second journey, and the swell, which was increasing rapidly, drove the boat on to the rocks, where one of the casks was slightly stove in. This accident proved later to be a serious one, since some sea-water had entered the cask and the contents were now brackish.

By midday the *James Caird* was ready for the voyage. Vincent and the carpenter had secured some dry clothes by exchange with members of the shore party (I heard afterwards that it was a full fortnight before the soaked garments were finally dried), and the boat's crew was standing by waiting for the order to cast off. A moderate westerly breeze was blowing. I went ashore in the *Stancomb Wills* and had a last word with Wild, who was remaining in full command, with directions as to his course of action in the event of our failure to bring relief, but I practically left the whole situation and scope of action and decision to his own judgment, secure in the knowledge that he would act wisely. I told him that I trusted the party to him and said good-bye to the men. Then we pushed off for the last time, and within a few minutes I was aboard the *James Caird*. The crew of the *Stancomb Wills* shook hands with us as the boats bumped together and offered us the last good wishes. Then, setting our jib, we cut the painter and moved away to the north-east. The men who were staying behind made a pathetic little group on the beach, with the grim heights of the island behind them and the sea seething at their feet, but they waved to us and gave three hearty cheers. There was hope in their hearts and they trusted us to bring the help that they needed.

I had all sails set, and the *James Caird* quickly dipped the beach and its line of dark figures. The westerly wind took us rapidly to the line of pack, and as we entered it I stood up with my arm around the mast, directing the steering, so as to avoid the great lumps of ice that were flung about in the heave of the sea. The pack thickened and we were forced to turn almost due east, running before the wind towards a gap I had seen in the morning from the high ground. I could not see the gap now, but we had come out on its bearing and I was prepared to find that it had been influenced by the easterly drift. At four o'clock in the afternoon we found the channel, much narrower than it had seemed in the morning but still navigable. Dropping sail, we rowed through without touching the ice anywhere, and by 5:30 p.m. we were clear of the pack with open water before us. We passed one more piece of ice in the darkness an hour later, but the pack lay behind, and with a fair wind swelling the sails we steered our little craft through the night, our hopes centred on our distant goal. The swell was very heavy now, and when the time came for our first evening meal we found great difficulty in keeping the Primus lamp alight and preventing the hoosh splashing out of the pot. Three men were needed to attend to the cooking, one man holding the lamp and two men guarding the aluminum cooking-pot, which had to be lifted clear of the Primus whenever the movement of the boat threatened to cause a disaster. Then the lamp had to be protected from water, for sprays were coming over the bows and our flimsy decking was by no means water-tight. All these operations were conducted in the confined space under the decking, where the men lay or knelt and adjusted themselves as best they could to the angles of our cases and ballast. It was uncomfortable, but we found consolation in the reflection that without the decking we could not have used the cooker at all.

The tale of the next sixteen days is one of supreme strife amid heaving waters. The sub-Antarctic Ocean lived up to its evil winter reputation. I decided to run north for at least two days while the wind held and so get into warmer weather before turning to the east and laying a course for South Georgia. We took two-hourly spells at the tiller. The men who were not on watch crawled into the sodden sleeping-bags and tried to forget their troubles for a period; but there was no comfort in the boat. The bags and cases seemed to be alive in the unfailing knack of presenting their most uncomfortable angles to our rest-seeking bodies. A man might imagine for a moment that he had found a position of ease, but always discovered quickly that some unyielding point was impinging on muscle or bone. The first night aboard the boat was one of acute discomfort for us all, and we were heartily glad when the dawn came and we could set about the preparation of a hot breakfast. . . .

A severe south-westerly gale on the fourth day out forced us to heave to. I would have liked to have run before the wind, but the sea was very high and the *James Caird* was in danger of broaching to and swamping. The delay was vexatious, since up to that time we had been making sixty or seventy miles a day; good going with our limited sail area. We hove to under double-reefed mainsail and our little jigger, and waited for the gale to blow itself out. During that afternoon we saw bits of wreckage, the remains probably of some unfortunate vessel that had failed to weather the strong gales south of Cape Horn. The weather conditions did not improve, and on the fifth day out the gale was so fierce that we were compelled to take in the double-reefed mainsail and hoist our small jib instead. We put out a sea-anchor to keep the *James Caird's* head up to the sea. This anchor consisted of a triangular canvas bag fastened to the end of the painter and allowed to stream out from the bows. The boat was high enough to catch the wind, and, as she drifted to leeward, the drag of the anchor kept her head to windward. Thus our boat took most of the seas more or less end on. Even then the crests of the waves often would curl right over us and we shipped a great deal of water, which necessitated unceasing bailing and pumping. Looking out abeam, we would see a hollow like a tunnel formed as the crest of a big wave toppled over on to the swelling body of water. A thousand times it appeared as though the *James Caird* must be engulfed; but the boat lived. The south-westerly gale had its birthplace above the Antarctic Continent, and its freezing breath lowered the temperature far towards zero. The sprays froze upon the boat and gave bows, sides, and decking a heavy coat of mail. This accumulation of ice reduced the buoyancy of the boat, and to that extent was an added peril; but it possessed a notable advantage from one point of view. The water ceased to drop and trickle from the canvas, and the spray came in solely at the well in the after part of the boat. We could not allow the load of ice to grow beyond a certain point, and in turns we crawled about the decking forward, chipping and picking at it with the available tools.

When daylight came on the morning of the sixth day out we saw and felt that the *James Caird* had lost her resiliency. She was not rising to the oncoming seas. The weight of the ice that had formed in her and upon her during the night was having its effect, and she was becoming more like a log than a boat. The situation called for immediate action. We first broke away the spare oars, which were encased in ice and frozen to the sides of the boat, and threw them overboard. We retained two oars for use when we got inshore. Two of the fur sleeping-bags went over the side; they were thoroughly wet, weighing probably 40 lb. each, and they had frozen stiff during the night. Three men constituted the watch below, and when a man went down it was better to turn into the wet bag just vacated by another man than to thaw out a frozen bag with the heat of his unfortunate body. We now had four bags, three in use and one for emergency use in case a member of the party should break down permanently. The reduction of weight relieved the boat to some extent, and vigorous chipping and scraping did more. We had to be very careful not to put axe or knife through the frozen canvas of the decking as we crawled over it, but gradually we got rid of a lot

ABOVE: Sir Ernest Shackleton (nearest flag) and his party at the South Pole, 1909 (*Polar Photos, London*)
BELOW: Admiral Richard E. Byrd alone at Advance Base in 1934 (*Office of Richard E. Byrd*)

Admiral Byrd is greeted by President Roosevelt, May 10, 1935, as the explorer returns from his fourth Polar expedition.

(*Office of Richard E. Byrd*)

ABOVE: Colonel Ewart S. Grogan *(From "From the Cape to Cairo" by E. S. Grogan and A. H. Sharp)*
BELOW: An early photograph of a pioneer safari *(F. H. Clarke)*

Captain Cousteau swims underwater with his
pressurized camera *(Jean de Wouters d'Oplinter)*

One of Cousteau's assistants diving toward a shark
(Jean de Wouters d'Oplinter)

ABOVE: The snow-capped peaks of the Andes
(Brian Fawcett)
BELOW: A stretch of the Tahuamanu river near
Porvenir in Bolivia *(Brian Fawcett)*

Colonel Lindbergh with his airplane, "Spirit of
St. Louis" *(Wide World Photo)*

English throngs greet Lindbergh at Croydon Field, 1927 *(Wide World Photo)*

Kon-Tiki ready to start in Callao Harbor
(From "Kon-Tiki" by Thor Heyerdahl)

On the way to Norbulingka! (*From "Seven Years in Tibet" by Heinrich Harrer*)

The Dalai Lama with his closest attendants *(From "Seven Years in Tibet" by Heinrich Harrer)*

ABOVE: Norbert Casteret entering the great shaft *(Norbert Casteret)*

BELOW: Gouffre de la Pierre Saint-Martin; the shake-hole *(Norbert Casteret)*

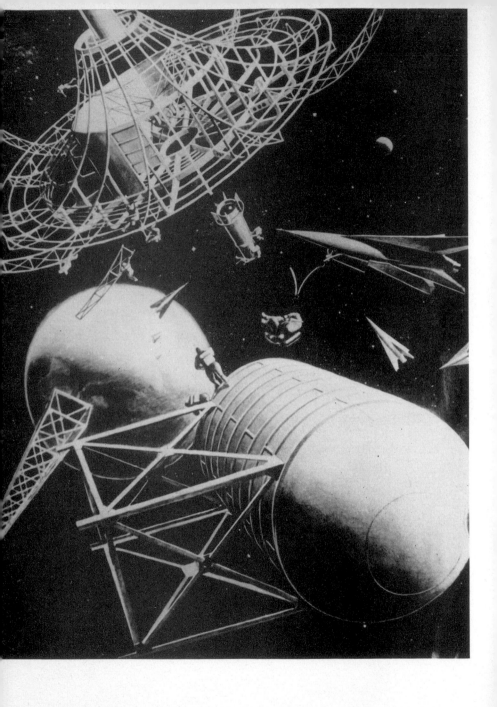

Building the Space Station (*R. A. Smith*)

of ice. The *James Caird* lifted to the endless waves as though she lived again.

About 11 a.m. the boat suddenly fell off into the trough of the sea. The painter had parted and the sea-anchor had gone. This was serious. The *James Caird* went away to leeward, and we had no chance at all of recovering the anchor and our valuable rope, which had been our only means of keeping the boat's head up to the seas without the risk of hoisting sail in a gale. Now we had to set the sail and trust to its holding. While the *James Caird* rolled heavily in the trough, we beat the frozen canvas until the bulk of the ice had cracked off it and then hoisted it. The frozen gear worked protestingly, but after a struggle our little craft came up to the wind again, and we breathed more freely. Skin frost-bites were troubling us, and we had developed large blisters on our fingers and hands. I shall always carry the scar of one of these frost-bites on my left hand, which became badly inflamed after the skin had burst and the cold had bitten deeply.

We held the boat up to the gale during that day, enduring as best we could discomforts that amounted to pain. The boat tossed interminably on the big waves under grey, threatening skies. Our thoughts did not embrace much more than the necessities of the hour. Every surge of the sea was an enemy to be watched and circumvented. We ate our scanty meals, treated our frost-bites, and hoped for the improved conditions that the morrow might bring. Night fell early, and in the lagging hours of darkness we were cheered by a change for the better in the weather. The wind dropped, the snow-squalls became less frequent, and the sea moderated. When the morning of the seventh day dawned there was not much wind. We shook the reef out of the sail and laid our course once more for South Georgia. The sun came out bright and clear, and presently Worsley got a snap for longitude. We hoped that the sky would remain clear until noon, so that we could get the latitude. We had been six days

out without an observation, and our dead reckoning naturally was uncertain. The boat must have presented a strange
appearance that morning. All hands basked in the sun. We
hung our sleeping bags to the mast and spread our socks and
other gear all over the deck. Some of the ice had melted off
the *James Caird* in the early morning after the gale began to
slacken, and dry patches were appearing in the decking.
Porpoises came blowing round the boat, and Cape pigeons
wheeled and swooped within a few feet of us. These little
black-and-white birds have an air of friendliness that is not
possessed by the great circling albatross. They had looked
grey against the swaying sea during the storm as they darted
about over our heads and uttered their plaintive cries. The
albatrosses, of the black or sooty variety, had watched with
hard, bright eyes, and seemed to have a quite impersonal
interest in our struggle to keep afloat amid the battering seas.
In addition to the Cape pigeons an occasional stormy petrel
flashed overhead. . . .

The eighth, ninth, and tenth days of the voyage had few
features worthy of special note. The wind blew hard during
those days, and the strain of navigating the boat was unceasing, but always we made some advance towards our goal.
No bergs showed on our horizon, and we knew that we were
clear of the ice-fields. Each day brought its little round of
troubles, but also compensation in the form of food and
growing hope. We felt that we were going to succeed. The
odds against us had been great, but we were winning
through. We still suffered severely from the cold, for, though
the temperature was rising, our vitality was declining owing
to shortage of food, exposure, and the necessity of maintain-
ing our cramped positions day and night. I found that it was
now absolutely necessary to prepare hot milk for all hands
during the night, in order to sustain life till dawn. This meant
lighting the Primus lamp in the darkness and involved an increased drain on our small store of matches. It was the rule

that one match must serve when the Primus was being lit. We had no lamp for the compass and during the early days of the voyage we would strike a match when the steersman wanted to see the course at night; but later the necessity for strict economy impressed itself upon us, and the practice of striking matches at night was stopped. We had one water-tight tin of matches. . . .

On the tenth night Worsley could not straighten his body after his spell at the tiller. He was thoroughly cramped, and we had to drag him beneath the decking and massage him before he could unbend himself and get into a sleeping-bag. A hard north-westerly gale came up on the eleventh day (May 5) and shifted to the south-west in the late afternoon. The sky was overcast and occasional snow-squalls added to the discomfort produced by a tremendous cross-sea—the worst, I thought, that we had experienced. At midnight I was at the tiller and suddenly noticed a line of clear sky between the south and south-west. I called to the other men that the sky was clearing, and then a moment later I realized that what I had seen was not a rift in the clouds but the white crest of an enormous wave. During twenty-six years' experience of the ocean in all its moods I had not encountered a wave so gigantic. It was a mighty upheaval of the ocean, a thing quite apart from the big white-capped seas that had been our tireless enemies for many days. I shouted, "For God's sake, hold on! It's got us!" Then came a moment of suspense that seemed drawn out into hours. White surged the foam of the breaking sea around us. We felt our boat lifted and flung forward like a cork in breaking surf. We were in a seething chaos of tortured water; but somehow the boat lived through it, half-full of water, sagging to the dead weight and shuddering under the blow. We baled with the energy of men fighting for life, flinging the water over the sides with every receptacle that came to our hands, and after ten minutes of uncertainty we felt the boat renew her life beneath us. She floated again and ceased to lurch drunkenly as though dazed by the attack of the sea. Earnestly we hoped that never again would we encounter such a wave.

The conditions in the boat, uncomfortable before, had been made worse by the deluge of water. All our gear was thoroughly wet again. Our cooking-stove had been floating about in the bottom of the boat, and portions of our last hoosh seemed to have permeated everything. Not until 3 a.m. when we were all chilled almost to the limit of endurance, did we manage to get the stove alight and make ourselves hot drinks. The carpenter was suffering particularly, but he showed grit and spirit. . . .

The weather was better on the following day (May 6), and we got a glimpse of the sun. Worsley's observation showed that we were not more than a hundred miles from the north-west corner of South Georgia. Two more days with a favourable wind and we would sight the promised land. I hoped that there would be no delay, for our supply of water was running very low. The hot drink at night was essential, but I decided that the daily allowance of water must be cut down to half a pint per man. The lumps of ice we had taken aboard had gone long ago. We were dependent upon the water we had brought from Elephant Island, and our thirst was increased by the fact that we were now using the brackish water in the breaker that had been slightly stove in in the surf when the boat was being loaded. Some sea-water had entered at that time.

Thirst took possession of us. I dared not permit the allowance of water to be increased since an unfavourable wind might drive us away from the island and lengthen our voyage by many days. Lack of water is always the most severe privation that men can be condemned to endure, and we found, as during our earlier boat voyage, that the salt water in our clothing and the salt spray that lashed our faces made our thirst grow quickly to a burning pain. I had to be very firm in refusing to allow any one to anticipate the morrow's allowance, which I was sometimes begged to do. We did the necessary work dully and hoped for the land. I had altered the course to the east so as to make sure of our striking the island, which would have been impossible to regain if we had run past the northern end. The course was laid on our scrap of chart for a point some thirty miles down the coast. That day and the following day passed for us in a sort of nightmare. Our mouths were dry and our tongues were swollen. The wind was still strong and the heavy sea forced us to navigate carefully, but any thought of our peril from the waves was buried beneath the consciousness of our raging thirst. The bright moments were those when we each received our one mug of hot milk during the long, bitter watches of the night. Things were bad for us in those days, but the end was coming. The morning of May 8 broke thick and stormy, with squalls from the north-west. We searched the waters ahead for a sign of land, and though we could see nothing more than had met our eyes for many days, we were cheered by a sense that the goal was near at hand. About ten o'clock that morning we passed a little bit of kelp, a glad signal of the proximity of land. An hour later we saw two shags sitting on a big mass of kelp, and knew then that we must be within ten or fifteen miles of the shore. These birds are as sure an indication of the proximity of land as a lighthouse is, for they never venture far to sea. We gazed ahead with increasing eagerness, and at 12:30 p.m., through a rift in the clouds, McCarthy caught a glimpse of the black cliffs of South Georgia, just fourteen days after our departure from Elephant Island. It was a glad moment. Thirst-ridden, chilled, and weak as we were, happiness irradiated us. The job was nearly done.

We stood in towards the shore to look for a landing-place, and presently we could see the green tussock-grass on the ledges above the surf-beaten rocks. Ahead of us and to the south, blind rollers showed the presence of uncharted reefs along the coast. Here and there the hungry rocks were close to the surface, and over them the great waves broke, swirling viciously and spouting thirty and forty feet into the air. The rocky coast appeared to descend sheer to the sea. Our need of water and rest was wellnigh desperate, but to have attempted a landing at that time would have been suicidal. Night was drawing near, and the weather indications were not favourable. There was nothing for it but to haul off till the following morning, so we stood away on the starboard tack until we had made what appeared to be a safe offing. Then we hove to in the high westerly swell. The hours passed slowly as we waited the dawn, which would herald, we fondly hoped, the last stage of our journey. Our thirst was a torment and we could scarcely touch our food; the cold seemed to strike right through our weakened bodies. At 5 a.m. the wind shifted to the north-west and quickly increased to one of the worst hurricanes any of us had ever experienced. A great cross-sea was running, and the wind simply shrieked as it tore the tops off the waves and converted the whole sea-scape into a haze of driving spray. Down into valleys, up to tossing heights, straining until her seams opened, swung our little boat, brave still but labouring heavily. We knew that the wind and set of the sea was driving us ashore, but we could do nothing. The dawn showed us a storm-torn ocean, and the morning passed without bringing us a sight of land; but at 1 p.m., through a rift in the flying mists, we got a glimpse of the huge crags of the island and realized that our position had become desperate. We were on a dead lee shore, and we could gauge our approach to the unseen cliffs by the roar of the breakers against the sheer walls of rock. I ordered the double-reefed mainsail to be set in the hope that we might claw off, and this attempt increased the strain upon the boat. The *James Caird* was bumping heavily, and the water was pouring in everywhere. Our thirst was forgotten in the realization of our imminent danger, as we baled unceasingly, and adjusted our weights from time to time; occasional glimpses showed that the shore was nearer. I knew that Annewkow Island lay to the south of us, but our small and badly marked chart showed uncertain reefs in the passage between the island and the mainland, and I dared not trust it, though as a last resort we could try to lie under the lee of the island. The afternoon wore away as we edged down the coast, with the thunder of the breakers in our ears. The approach of evening found us still some distance from Annewkow Island, and, dimly in the twilight, we could see a snow-capped mountain looming above us. The chance of surviving the night, with the driving gale and the implacable sea forcing us on to the lee shore, seemed small. I think most of us had a feeling that the end was very near. Just after 6 p.m., in the dark, as the boat was in the yeasty backwash from the seas flung from this iron-bound coast, then, just when things looked their worst, they changed for the best. I have marvelled often at the thin line that divides success from failure and the sudden turn that leads from apparently certain disaster to comparative safety. The wind suddenly shifted, and we were free once more to make an offing. Almost as soon as the gale eased, the pin that locked the mast to the thwart fell out. It must have been on the point of doing this throughout the hurricane, and if it had gone nothing could have saved us; the mast would have snapped like a carrot. Our backstays had carried away once before when iced up and were not too strongly fastened now. We were thankful indeed for the mercy that had held that pin in its place throughout the hurricane.

We stood off shore again, tired almost to the point of apathy. Our water had long been finished. The last was about a pint of hairy liquid, which we strained through a bit of gauze from the medicine-chest. The pangs of thirst attacked us with redoubled intensity, and I felt that we must make a

landing on the following day at almost any hazard. The night
wore on. We were very tired. We longed for day. When at
last the dawn came on the morning of May 10 there was practically no wind, but a high cross-sea was running. We made
slow progress towards the shore. About 8 a.m. the wind
backed to the north-west and threatened another blow. We
had sighted in the meantime a big indentation which I
thought must be King Haakon Bay, and I decided that we
must land there. We set the bows of the boat towards the
bay and ran before the freshening gale. Soon we had angry
reefs on either side. Great glaciers came down to the sea and
offered no landing-place. The sea spouted on the reefs and
thundered against the shore. About noon we sighted a line of
jagged reef, like blackened teeth, that seemed to bar the
entrance to the bay. Inside, comparatively smooth water
stretched eight or nine miles to the head of the bay. A gap in
the reef appeared, and we made for it. But the fates had another rebuff for us. The wind shifted and blew from the east
right out of the bay. We could see the way through the reef,
but we could not approach it directly. That afternoon we
bore up, tacking five times in the strong wind. The last tack
enabled us to get through, and at last we were in the wide
mouth of the bay. Dusk was approaching. A small cove, with
a boulder-strewn beach guarded by a reef, made a break in
the cliffs on the south side of the bay, and we turned in that
direction. I stood in the bows directing the steering as we
ran through the kelp and made the passage of the reef. The
entrance was so narrow that we had to take in the oars, and
the swell was piling itself right over the reef into the cove;
but in a minute or two we were inside, and in the gathering
darkness the *James Caird* ran in on a swell and touched the
beach. I sprang ashore with the short painter and held on
when the boat went out with the backward surge. When the
James Caird came in again three of the men got ashore, and
they held the painter while I climbed some rocks with an-

other line. A slip on the wet rocks twenty feet up nearly closed my part of the story just at the moment when we were achieving safety. A jagged piece of rock held me and at the same time bruised me sorely. However, I made fast the line, and in a few minutes we were all safe on the beach, with the boat floating in the surging water just off the shore. We heard a gurgling sound that was sweet music in our ears, and, peering around, found a stream of fresh water almost at our feet. A moment later we were down on our knees drinking the pure ice-cold water in long draughts that put new life into us. It was a splendid moment.

BLIZZARD IN ANTARCTICA

(From ALONE. New York: G. P. Putnam's Sons, 1938)

The late Rear Admiral Richard E. Byrd, U.S.N., one of America's great explorers, led five major expeditions to Antarctica over a period of almost thirty years. During the Antarctic winter of 1934, Admiral Byrd left his expedition's base at Little America to man alone an advanced weather observation base "planted in the dark immensity of the Ross Ice Barrier, on a line between Little America and the South Pole. It was the first inland weather station ever occupied in the world's southernmost continent." In this remote outpost, Admiral Byrd lived for almost seven months in a tiny shack some fifteen feet long and eleven feet wide, its walls buried in the snow. For five months of this time he was completely alone. Equipped with meteorological instruments and radio for communication with Little America, the shack was entered from the surface of the snow by a trap door in one corner of a two-foot projection of one side of the roof. This projection formed an open space between the wall of the shack and the opposite wall of snow. The shack door opened into this space, which Admiral Byrd called his "verandah." Ventilation was by means of pipes leading to the outside air. Much of Admiral Byrd's vigil at Bolling Advance Weather Base was a terrible ordeal because of physical illness caused by fumes from the stove, lamps, and generator motor. In the following passage Admiral Byrd relates a dramatic experience which occurred shortly before he became critically ill from the fumes, and describes a blizzard as seen by the southernmost man in the world.

The night was settling down in earnest. By May 17th, one month after the sun had sunk below the horizon, the noon twilight was dwindling to a mere chink in the darkness, lit by a cold reddish glow. Days when the wind brooded in the north or east, the Barrier became a vast stagnant shadow surmounted by swollen masses of clouds, one layer of darkness piled on top of the other. This was the polar night, the morbid countenance of the Ice Age. Nothing moved; nothing was visible. This was the soul of inertness. One could almost hear a distant creaking as if a great weight were settling.

Out of the deepening darkness came the cold. On May 19th, when I took the usual walk, the temperature was 65° below zero. For the first time the canvas boots failed to protect my feet. One heel was nipped, and I was forced to return to the hut and change to reindeer mukluks. That day I felt miserable; my body was racked by shooting pains—exactly as if I had been gassed. Very likely I was; in inspecting the ventilator pipes next morning I discovered that the intake pipe was completely clogged with rime and that the outlet pipe was two-thirds full. Next day—Sunday the 20th—was the coldest yet. The minimum thermometer dropped to 72° below zero; the inside thermograph, which always read a bit lower than the instruments in the shelter, stood at—74°; and the thermograph in the shelter was stopped dead—the ink, though well laced with glycerine, and the lubricant were both frozen. So violently did the air in the fuel tank expand after the stove was lit that oil went shooting all over the place; to insulate the tank against similar temperature spreads I wrapped around it the rubber air cushion which by some lucky error had been included among my gear. In the glow of a flashlight the vapor rising from the stovepipe and the outlet ventilator looked like the discharge from two steam engines. My fingers agonized over the thermograph, and I was hours putting it to rights. The fuel wouldn't flow from the drums; I had to take one inside and heat it near the stove. All day long I kept two primus stoves burning in the tunnel.

Sunday the 20th also brought a radio schedule; I had the devil's own time trying to meet it. The engine balked for an hour; my fingers were so brittle and frostbitten from tinkering with the carburetor that, when I actually made contact with Little America, I could scarcely work the key. "Ask Haines come on," was my first request. While Hutcheson searched the tunnels of Little America for the Senior Meteorologist, I chatted briefly with Charlie Murphy. Little America claimed only −60°. "But we're moving the brass monkeys below," Charlie advised. "Seventy-one below here now," I said. "You can have it," was the closing comment from the north.

Then Bill Haines's merry voice sounded in the earphones. I explained the difficulty with the thermograph. "Same trouble we've had," Bill said. "It's probably due to frozen oil. I'd suggest you bring the instrument inside, and try soaking it in gasoline, to cut whatever oil traces remain. Then rinse it in ether. As for the ink's freezing, you might try adding more glycerine." Bill was in a jovial mood. "Look at me, Admiral," he boomed. "I never have any trouble with the instruments. The trick is in having an ambitious and docile assistant." I really chuckled over that because I knew, from the first expedition, what Grimminger, the Junior Meteorologist, was going through: Bill, with his back to the fire and blandishment on his tongue, persuading the recruit that duty and the opportunity for self-improvement required him to go up into the blizzard to fix a balky trace; Bill humming to himself in the warmth of a shack while the assistant in an open pit kept a theodolite trained on the sounding balloon soaring into the night, and stuttered into a telephone the different vernier readings from which Bill was calculating the velocities and directions of the upper air currents. That day I rather wished that I, too, had an assistant. He would have taken his turn on the anenometer pole, no mistake. The frost in the iron cleats went through the fur soles of the mukluks, and froze the balls of my feet. My breath made little explosive sounds on the wind; my lungs, already sore, seemed to shrivel when I breathed.

Seldom had the aurora flamed more brilliantly. For hours the night danced to its frenetic excitement. And at times the sound of Barrier quakes was like that of heavy guns. My tongue was swollen and sore from drinking scalding hot tea, and the tip of my nose ached from frostbite. A big wind, I guessed, would come out of this still cold; it behooved me to look to my roof. I carried gallons of water topside and poured it around the edges of the shack. It froze almost as soon as it hit. The ice was an armor plating over the packed drift.

At midnight, when I clambered topside for an auroral "ob," a wild sense of suffocation came over me the instant I pushed my shoulders through the trapdoor. My lungs gasped, but no air reached them. Bewildered and perhaps a little frightened, I slid down the ladder and lunged into the shack. In the warm air the feeling passed as quickly as it had come. Curious but cautious, I again made my way up the ladder. And again the same thing happened; I lost my breath, but I perceived why. A light air was moving down from eastward; and its bitter touch, when I faced into it, was constricting the breathing passages. So I turned my face away from it, breathing into my glove; and in that attitude finished the "ob." Before going below, I made an interesting experiment. I put a thermometer on the snow, let it lie there awhile, and discovered that the temperature at the surface was actually 5° colder than at the level of the instrument shelter, four feet higher. Reading in the sleeping bag afterwards, I froze one finger, although I shifted the book steadily from one hand to the other, slipping the unoccupied hand into the warmth of the bag.

* * *

Out of the cold and out of the east came the wind. It came on gradually, as if the sheer weight of the cold were almost too much to be moved. On the night of the 21st the barometer started down. The night was black as a thunderhead when I made my first trip topside; and a tension in the wind, a bulking of shadows in the night indicated that a new storm center was forming. Next morning, glad of an excuse to stay underground, I worked a long time on the Escape Tunnel by the light of a red candle standing in a snow recess. That day I pushed the emergency exit to a distance of twenty-two feet, the farthest it was ever to go. My stint done, I sat down on a box, thinking how beautiful was the red of the candle, how white the rough-hewn snow. Soon I became aware of an increasing clatter of the anemometer cups. Realizing that the wind was picking up, I went topside to make sure that everything was secured. It is a queer experience to watch a blizzard rise. First there is the wind, rising out of nowhere. Then the Barrier unwrenches itself from quietude; and the surface, which just before had seemed as hard and polished as metal, begins to run like a making sea. Sometimes, if the wind strikes hard, the drift comes across the Barrier like a hurrying white cloud, tossed hundreds of feet in the air. Other times the growth is gradual. You become conscious of a general slithering movement on all sides. The air fills with tiny scraping and sliding and rustling sounds as the first loose crystals stir. In a little while they are moving as solidly as an incoming tide, which creams over the ankles, then surges to the waist, and finally is at the throat. I have walked in drift so thick as not to be able to see a foot ahead of me; yet, when I glanced up, I could see the stars shining through the thin layer just overhead.

Smoking tendrils were creeping up the anemometer pole when I finished my inspection. I hurriedly made the trapdoor fast, as a sailor might batten down a hatch; and knowing that my ship was well secured, I retired to the cabin to ride out the storm. It could not reach me, hidden deep in the Barrier crust; nevertheless the sounds came down. The gale sobbed in the ventilators, shook the stovepipe until I thought it would be jerked out by the roots, pounded the roof with sledgehammer blows. I could actually feel the suction effect through the pervious snow. A breeze flickered in the room and the tunnels. The candles wavered and went out. My only light was the feeble storm lantern.

Even so, I didn't have any idea how really bad it was until I went aloft for an observation. As I pushed back the trapdoor, the drift met me like a moving wall. It was only a few steps from the ladder to the instrument shelter, but it seemed more like a mile. The air came at me in snowy rushes; I breasted it as I might a heavy surf. No night had ever seemed so dark. The beam from the flashlight was choked in its throat; I could not see my hand before my face.

My windproofs were caked with drift by the time I got below. I had a vague feeling that something had changed while I was gone, but what, I couldn't tell. Presently I noticed that the shack was appreciably colder. Raising the stove lid, I was surprised to find that the fire was out, though the tank was half full. I decided that I must have turned off the valve unconsciously before going aloft; but, when I put a match to the burner, the draught down the pipe blew out the flame. The wind, then, must have killed the fire. I got it going again, and watched it carefully.

The blizzard vaulted to gale force. Above the roar the deep, taut thrumming note of the radio antenna and the anemometer guy wires reminded me of wind in a ship's rigging. The wind direction trace turned scratchy on the sheet; no doubt drift had short-circuited the electric contacts, I decided. Realizing that it was hopeless to attempt to try to keep them clear, I let the instrument be. There were other ways of getting the wind direction. I tied a handkerchief to a bamboo pole and ran it through the outlet ventilator; with a flashlight I could tell which way the cloth was whipped. I did this at hourly intervals, noting any change of direction on the sheet. But by 2 o'clock in the morning I had had enough of this periscope sighting. If I expected to sleep and at the same time maintain the continuity of the records, I had no choice but to clean the contact points.

The wind was blowing hard then. The Barrier shook from the concussions overhead; and the noise was as if the entire physical world were tearing itself to pieces. I could scarcely heave the trapdoor open. The instant it came clear I was plunged into a blinding smother. I came out crawling, clinging to the handle of the door until I made sure of my bearings. Then I let the door fall shut, not wanting the tunnel filled with drift. To see was impossible. Millions of tiny pellets exploded in my eyes, stinging like BB shot. It was even hard to breathe, because snow instantly clogged the mouth and nostrils. I made my way toward the anemometer pole on hands and knees, scared that I might be bowled off my feet if I stood erect; one false step and I should be lost forever.

I found the pole all right; but not until my head collided with a cleat. I managed to climb it, too, though ten million ghosts were tearing at me, ramming their thumbs into my eyes. But the errand was useless. Drift as thick as this would mess up the contact points as quickly as they were cleared; besides, the wind cups were spinning so fast that I stood a good chance of losing a couple of fingers in the process. Coming down the pole, I had a sense of being whirled violently through the air, with no control over my movements. The trapdoor was completely buried when I found it again, after scraping around for some time with my mittens. I pulled at the handle, first with one hand, then with both. It did not give. It's a tight fit, anyway, I mumbled to myself. The drift has probably wedged the corners. Standing astride the hatch, I braced myself and heaved with all my strength. I might just as well have tried hoisting the Barrier.

Panic took me then, I must confess. Reason fled. I clawed at the three-foot square of timber like a madman. I beat on it with my fists, trying to shake the snow loose; and, when that did no good, I lay flat on my belly and pulled until my hands went weak from cold and weariness. Then I crooked my elbow, put my face down, and said over and over again, You damn fool, you damn fool. Here for weeks I had been defending myself against the danger of being penned inside the shack; instead, I was now locked out; and nothing could be worse, especially since I had only a wool parka and pants under my windproofs. Just two feet below was sanctuary— warmth, food, tools, all the means of survival. All these things were an arm's length away, but I was powerless to reach them.

There is something extravagantly insensate about an Antarctic blizzard at night. Its vindictiveness cannot be measured on an anemometer sheet. It is more than just wind; it is a solid wall of snow moving at gale force, pounding like surf.* The whole malevolent rush is concentrated upon you as upon a personal enemy. In the senseless explosion of sound you are reduced to a crawling thing on the margin of a disintegrating world; you can't see, you can't hear, you can hardly move. The lungs gasp after the air is sucked out of them, and the brain is shaken. Nothing in the world will so quickly isolate a man.

Half-frozen, I stabbed toward one of the ventilators, a few feet away. My mittens touched something round and cold. Cupping it in my hands, I pulled myself up. This was the outlet ventilator. Just why, I don't know—but instinct made me kneel and press my face against the opening. Nothing in the room was visible, but a dim patch of light illuminated the floor, and warmth rose up to my face. That steadied me.

Still kneeling, I turned my back to the blizzard and considered what might be done. I thought of breaking in the windows in the roof, but they lay two feet down in hard crust, and were reinforced with wire besides. If I only had something to dig with, I could break the crust and stamp the windows in with my feet. The pipe cupped between my hands supplied the first inspiration; maybe I could use that to dig with. It, too, was wedged tight; I pulled until my arms

---

* Because of this blinding, suffocating drift, in the Antarctic winds of only moderate velocity have the punishing force of full-fledged hurricanes elsewhere.

ached, without budging it; I had lost all track of time, and the despairing thought came to me that I was lost in a task without an end. Then I remembered the shovel. A week before, after leveling drift from the last light blow, I had stabbed a shovel handle up in the crust somewhere to leeward. That shovel would save me. But how to find it in the avalanche of the blizzard?

I lay down and stretched out full length. Still holding the pipe, I thrashed around with my feet, but pummeled only empty air. Then I worked back to the hatch. The hard edges at the opening provided another grip, and again I stretched out and kicked. Again no luck. I dared not let go until I had something else familiar to cling to. My foot came up against the other ventilator pipe. I edged back to that, and from the new anchorage repeated the maneuver. This time my ankle struck something hard. When I felt it and recognized the handle, I wanted to caress it.

Embracing this thrice-blessed tool, I inched back to the trapdoor. The handle of the shovel was just small enough to pass under the little wooden bridge which served as a grip. I got both hands on the shovel and tried to wrench the door up; my strength was not enough, however. So I lay down flat on my belly and worked my shoulders under the shovel. Then I heaved, the door sprang open, and I rolled down the shaft. When I tumbled into the light and warmth of the room, I kept thinking, how wonderful, how perfectly wonderful.

COLONEL EWART S. GROGAN, GENTLEMAN ADVENTURER

(From TALES OF THE AFRICAN FRONTIER, by J. A. Hunter and
Daniel P. Mannix. New York: Harper & Brothers, 1954)

*One of the most daring achievements in the opening up of the African
frontier was Ewart S. Grogan's pioneer journey on foot in 1898-1899,
from the Cape Colony to Cairo. At the time when this resourceful
young explorer walked from one end of the Dark Continent to the
other, much of the country through which he passed was still unexplored and was infested with dangerous wild animals and hostile tribes.
Here is the story of Grogan's unusual exploit, as told by John A.
Hunter, the well-known white hunter of Kenya.*

In the winter of 1899, Captain Dunn, a British officer stationed in Egypt, took a small native craft and went on a
shooting and fishing trip along the Sobat River in the lower
Sudan. He stopped to camp one night on the shore. South of
him lay thousands of miles of jungle, swamps and desert, un-
mapped and unexplored. Captain Dunn's astonishment may
well be imagined when, the next morning, he saw coming out
of this wilderness a small group of porters, clearly at their
last gasp, led by a young Englishman with an unlit pipe in
his mouth and a sporting rifle slung over his shoulder. The
young man's face was swollen by mosquito bites, he was
flushed with fever, and he was clearly unable to use one arm.
The porters collapsed on the ground, but the stranger removed his pipe and bowed politely.

Their conversation has been recorded. It went like this:

Captain Dunn: "How do you do?"

The Stranger: "Oh, very fit, thanks. How are you? Had any sport?"

Captain Dunn: "Pretty fair. Have a drink? You must be hungry. I'll hurry on lunch. Had any shooting?"

But at lunch, the captain's English reserve gave way and he could not help blurting out, "Excuse me, but do you mind telling me where the devil you came from?"

"From the Cape," replied the stranger.

The Cape of Good Hope lay four thousand miles to the south—four thousand miles of country full of cannibal tribes, wild beasts and mountain ranges. It was generally considered well-nigh impassable. Captain Dunn may well have thought the young man delirious. Yet this was not the case. He had indeed made this amazing trek on foot, the first man in history to accomplish the feat.

The young man was Ewart S. Grogan, now Colonel Grogan, and I am proud to say he is a friend of mine. After his famous walk, he settled in Kenya and now has a magnificent farm near Taveta in the southern part of the colony. Although now in his eightieth year, the colonel is still as slim and straight as he was when he walked from the Cape to Cairo. A prominent figure in the government, he is equally famous for his great knowledge of African affairs and his biting wit. Although many stories could be told of him, I will confine this narrative to an account of his notable walk, which I consider one of the great feats of all time. I have based this story on the colonel's writings and he has been kind enough to fill in a number of details not mentioned in his diary of the trip.

The flip of a ha'penny started Ewart Grogan on his adventuresome career. His father, a prosperous land agent, sent the boy to Cambridge and after graduation, young Ewart decided to become an artist. His father, nothing loath, sent the boy to one of the best art schools in the country. But as Grogan now admits, "After being at the school awhile, I didn't particularly like the look of the kind of people who were artists." One day his bearded teacher held up a sketch the young man was working on and after examining it said impressively, "If you work for many years, living, dreaming, thinking nothing but art, art, art, then you may someday be a great artist." He waited for the young man to faint with joy.

"But I'm not sure that I want to be an artist," remarked Grogan. "I think that I'd rather be a policeman."

His teacher nearly exploded with rage. "I suggest you make up your mind," he snapped.

"Right you are," agreed Grogan. He pulled a ha'penny out of his pocket. "Heads, I become an artist. Tails, I become a policeman." He flipped the coin. It came down tails. "Sorry!" said Grogan politely. Getting his hat and coat, he left the studio never to return.

Grogan did indeed become a policeman but it was a policeman of a somewhat special sort. The Matabele Uprising had broken out in South Africa, one of the numerous native wars with which the British Empire was constantly plagued during the Victorian era, and Grogan enlisted as a trooper. He joined a gun crew and served as Number Four man on a muzzle-loading seven-pounder. After the war, Grogan returned to England so wasted by fever that the doctors thought he might never completely recover.

This was a sore blow to young Grogan, for during his tour of service in South Africa, he had met Cecil Rhodes and caught that remarkable man's dream of a British Africa, extending from Cape-town to the shores of the Mediterranean. Rhodes believed that the first requirement for linking the vast continent together was a railroad running down the spine of Africa, to open the interior to commerce. But was such a railroad possible? What mountain ranges would it have to cross, how many rivers, how many stretches of jungle and desert? Even more important, would it have to cut

across areas already parceled out among nations hostile to
Great Britain. It was Grogan's dream to make the long trek
from the Cape to Cairo and map a possible route for the proposed railway.

However, the doctors told the young man that he must
take a rest before even considering such an adventure. A
long sea voyage was advised, and Grogan decided to go to
New Zealand and stay with an old Cambridge chum who had
settled there. During the voyage, he studied books on engineering and surveying and by the time he arrived in New
Zealand, he had a rough knowledge of the subject.

His friend had an extremely pretty sister named Gertrude
Watt. She and Ewart Grogan fell in love. They planned mar-
riage but Miss Watt had a guardian who did not approve of
Ewart.

"Young man, you appear to be drifting down the river of
life without a rudder," the pompous old gentleman told
Grogan. "A girl in the position of my ward can expect to
marry an outstanding man."

Grogan reflected, "If I were to walk from the Cape to
Cairo, would you consider me sufficiently outstanding?"

The older man was not amused. "I can only suppose that
you are either a fool or have decided to play one. The jungles
of Central Africa are impassable. Stanley was able to get
about only on rivers and he had to take an armed guard of six
hundred men to fight off the native tribes. To traverse the
continent you would need a small army."

"Oh, hardly that," remarked Grogan. "If you have a large
group, you arouse suspicion. I believe a small party could get
through without too much trouble." This, then, might be said
to be the start of the famous walk. Grogan returned to England and a few months later sailed for South Africa in company with another young man named Arthur Henry Sharp,
who had decided to come along part of the way.

I should like here to say a few words about the typical

upper-middle-class young Englishman of the Victorian era, of which these two young men were fine examples. According to our modern standards, they were in many ways a pampered lot. It was taken for granted that they would attend the best schools and afterwards go to a famous university. The problem of making a living was a minor one, for their parents were usually well-off. They were a class born to command and to possessions. Yet there was another side to the lives of these young men which is now largely forgotten.

They were brought up under a code so strict that many today would regard it as just short of brutality. When still children, they were sent off to schools where the slightest infringement of the rules was punished by a cane in the hands of a master or a prefect. For a boy to shirk the roughest games or complain of the most savage bullying promptly condemned him as an effeminate sniveler. They were generally introduced to blood sports as soon as they could sit a horse or hold a gun and for many of them the seasons of the year were divided up according to what animal it was appropriate to hunt or shoot. To many people, this would seem a faulty upbringing but most of the young men grew up from childhood knowing how to handle a gun, how to endure hardship and how to put their horses at the most difficult hedge without flinching.

When Grogan and Sharp left on their memorable trip, they were already first-class shots. The habit of command was strong in them, and in dealing with savage and unruly porters this ability was worth more than all the beads and trinkets in Africa. There was still another side to their nature, also typical of the time. Although they could take only the barest essentials on such a trip, they included several volumes of poetry as naturally as they included ammunition for their guns.

The two young explorers differed strikingly in appearance. The pictures of Grogan show him as a slender, clean-shaven youth who always seemed to have a pipe stuck nonchalantly in the corner of his mouth. Sharp wore the mustache and carefully trimmed whiskers so fashionable among the young men of the period. He was a quieter, more matter-of-fact individual than Grogan but with an almost equal love of adventure. For equipment, they had a battery that consisted principally of two sporting magazine .303 rifles—weapons I would consider somewhat light for even the larger antelopes, but which in their hands served admirably for everything from ducks to elephants. Each man had a small tent, a camp cot, mosquito netting and a few changes of clothing. Their medical equipment was a bottle of quinine and another of potassium permanganate for wounds. The bulk of their outfit consisted of boxes of beads and rolls of the brightly colored cloth called "Americani," manufactured in the United States and used as a standard form of currency among African tribes. They also took along cameras and surveying instruments. Although they had some supplies, they intended to rely mainly on their rifles to provide food for the expedition.

In February, 1898, the two young men arrived in South Africa and began their memorable trek. The beginning of the trip across the great, open plains of the veldt proved reasonably easy yet it was here that they first encountered African big game. One afternoon while Grogan and Sharp were fishing, they were attacked by a buffalo. Grogan promptly dove into the stream in reckless disregard of the crocodile-infested waters. Sharp, who had no idea of the power of a buffalo, stood his ground. As coolly as though firing at a target on a rifle range, he put bullet after bullet into the oncoming bull. As he was using soft-nosed .303's, the odds were a hundred to one on the buffalo. But one of his shots broke the bull's jaw. The buffalo staggered and Sharp fired again, breaking the animal's fetlock. The buffalo rolled to within three yards of the young man who was then able to finish him off. As Grogan emerged dripping from the stream, Sharp said to him in tones of mild surprise, "I had no idea these animals could take so much punishment. Next time one charges me, I'll follow your example and get out of his way."

So far, the young men had been able to travel by ox wagon and mule-drawn carts. But when they reached Salisbury in southern Rhodesia, there was no other means of transportation north except their own feet, and equipment had to be carried by porters. Generally, native porters refused to travel more than a few miles from their village. In each new district it was necessary to pay off the old group and hire a new batch. However, a few miles north of Salisbury, the young men were fortunate enough to hire some Watonga porters who had a taste for adventure. Four of these porters stayed with Grogan all the way to Cairo. He assured the porters that he would show them great mountains that spit fire and passes so high that water turned to stone. Grogan always claimed that the Watonga went with him mainly because they didn't want to miss the chance of being with such a talented liar.

The safari pressed northward until by April they reached Ujiji on Lake Tanganyika where Stanley had found Livingstone thirty years before. Tanganyika was now a German protectorate, but there were still a number of old Arabs in the town who had settled there in the days of Tippu Tib. Slavery had been abolished, but these elderly men were still being cared for by their old slaves who had refused freedom. Ahead of the young men lay a series of mountain ranges which the old Arabs assured them were impassable. But Grogan and Sharp determined to make the attempt. As there would be no game in the mountains, all food for the expedition would have to be carried by porters. They hired 130 rough-looking local natives who said they were willing to go. Grogan and Sharp organized ten of their Watonga porters into a sort of tiny standing army to handle this wild crew and started across the range.

Trouble began almost immediately. The nights were so cold that the porters, used to the heavy heat of the lowlands, sat shivering around their campfires unable to get warm. The Watonga felt the change even more than the new porters. The expedition crossed a ridge seven thousand feet high, and the next morning two of the Watonga deserted. This was a particularly serious blow as Grogan and Sharp had looked on the Watonga as the noncommissioned officers of their little force.

The weather constantly grew worse. Every morning dawned with the mountains covered by a cold, dank mist. The men had to force their way through masses of mimosa bushes heavy with dew. Within a few minutes, every man was as completely soaked as though he'd been under a shower. As the mist usually did not lift until afternoon, no one ever had a chance to get properly dried out. Sharp was bitten so badly by mosquitoes that his hands became infected and he could scarcely use them. Both he and Grogan began to have constant attacks of fever which they could not throw off because of the chill and constant wetting.

Then the ten Watonga who had served as guards deserted in a body. Sharp came down with blackwater fever. Grogan was semi-delirious with malaria and running a temperature of 106.9. The two boys nursed each other and struggled on until they finally crossed the range and dropped into a little valley on the other side. Ahead of them a new range of mountains stretched on, apparently endlessly, but in the valley was a small native village. Here they stopped—collapsed would be a better term—while their porters returned to Ujiji, leaving Grogan and Sharp with the last four of the Watonga.

They stayed in the village for several weeks. Grogan was in a "pitiable condition," as he wrote in his journal, and Sharp, although very little better, acted as nurse. Ahead of them lay unknown country, the first completely unexplored territory they had reached. "Our expedition was really only just beginning and yet there I was, dying before the trip had actually started," Grogan told me. For days, the boy lay on his cot looking at that great sea of mountains ahead of him, some of the most magnificent scenery in all Africa. Somewhere beyond those ridges lay the great Kivu Lake and the volcanoes reported by earlier explorers who had come in from the East Coast. Whether or not it was possible to reach Kivu from the south still remained to be seen.

Grogan did not recover as rapidly as they had hoped. The intense, mucky heat of the valley seemed to augment his fever. At last, it was decided to push on and see if he would not do better in the cool highlands. As he was too weak to walk, Sharp arranged to have him carried in a litter. A new group of porters was hired and the boys headed out across the valley toward the distant ridges.

I doubt if any other country in the world shows such sharp variations in climate as Africa. Central Africa is tropical but in the highlands a man can walk for days through great forests and swear that he is in Canada or Norway. Then, within a space of a few hours, he drops down into a valley full of plam trees and grass huts where elephants roam and the streams are full of crocodiles. By the next morning, he may be crossing a desert where the only sign of life is an occasional lizard. That night he may reach a plateau region that closely resembles the English countryside—pleasant grasslands cut up by little streams flowing gently between green banks. In another day or two he may be floundering through papyrus swamps, being eaten alive by mosquitoes and listening to the bellow of hippos in the reeds around him.

In the next few weeks, Grogan and Sharp passed through all these types of country and many more. They saw their first elephant. Grogan left his litter to stalk one big bull—he was still so weak that his porters followed him with the litter in case he fainted—but the elephant escaped. Then the expedition entered a well-inhabited prosperous district. Great herds of cattle with enormous horns grazed on the mountain slopes, guarded by naked children who hardly came up to the beasts' bellies. In the lowlands were forests of banana trees, carefully cultivated. Women, nude to the waist, worked in the fields of peas and beans. As they approached the shores of Lake Kivu, Ngenzi, the king of the district, came out to greet them. He even accompanied them for several miles with his retinue as a gesture of friendship.

When the king had left, the young men proceeded to check their stores and discovered to their horror that the king had not departed empty-handed. Much of their precious clothing had been stolen, but this was a minor matter. A tin box had been taken, containing their sextants, artificial horizon, thermometers and many of their records and photographs. In a few minutes, much of the hard work of the last months had been lost and the value of the rest of the trip seriously curtailed.

The old chief foolishly hung about the outskirts of the safari, hoping for another windfall. The young men explained to him how important the missing articles were, but the chief professed complete ignorance of the whole affair. "There are many bad men in this country," he explained blandly, "I can't keep track of them."

Grogan and Sharp may have had many shortcomings, but indecision was not one of them. The astonished chief suddenly found himself looking down the muzzles of two rifles. Before he could protest, he was grabbed by the scruff of the neck and flung into the boys' tent. When his bodyguard moved in to rescue him, they were also confronted by the two steady guns. After thinking the matter over, the bodyguard decided to let the chief stay where he was.

After bitterly protesting his innocence, the chief finally asked to speak to some of his officials. He gave them a few orders and the men left, returning shortly with the boys' missing clothes. Grogan and Sharp demanded their records and instruments, but the chief denied all knowledge of them.

Then the explorers had an inspiration. The natives obviously cared little about the chief, but they were vitally
interested in the welfare of their cattle. Leaving Sharp to
guard the camp, Grogan took a small force of the porters
and set out for the nearest village. There he and his men
seized a herd of 190 cattle and started driving them back
to camp. Within a few minutes, the alarm drums sounded
and hundreds of armed warriors began to assemble on the
hills. Through the guide-interpreter, the young men shouted
to the warriors that they would return the cattle as soon as
the contents of the tin box were returned.

The next morning, the tribesmen sent in a deputation. "We
have already returned your clothes and those were the only
valuable things we took from you," they explained. "The
other articles were worthless—you couldn't wear them, you
couldn't eat them, you couldn't cook your food with them.
So we threw them down a crevice in the hills. They are gone
for good, and even if you shoot the chief and take all the
cattle in the country you can never get them back. Now
please go away and leave us alone."

Brokenhearted and miserable, the boys could do nothing
else. They could only make a resolve never to allow the instruments and records still remaining to get out of their sight
even for a moment.

The expedition passed through the country of the Watusi,
the giant men who average over seven feet in height and
have for their slaves the Wahutu, the original inhabitants of
the district. Although the Wahutu outnumbered their giant
masters a hundred to one, they regarded them with almost
superstitious awe and never questioned their authority. A
few marches farther on, the young men saw their first pyg-
mies, little men scarcely four feet tall who live on the borders
of the giants' country.

So far, Grogan and Sharp had been concerned about the

natives' stealing from their porters. Now they ran into the problem of how to keep the porters from stealing from the natives. They passed through districts so poor that the porters could hire the local inhabitants to carry their loads for them. The average wage for a native at that time was three shillings a month (about seventy-five cents). For a few pennies, the porters were able to employ helpers. Then as the safari passed through still more poverty-stricken areas, the substitutes hired substitutes, who in turn hired other substitutes until the load was finally carried by a small boy or a starving old man while the original porter and two or three "middlemen" walked alongside like gentlemen of leisure. The young Englishmen did not feel it was their responsibility to interfere with this system as long as everyone was satisfied, but soon they received complaints from local chiefs that the idle porters were raiding villages, molesting girls and looting houses. It must be remembered that one of the old foot safaris often stretched out for miles. The men were constantly stopping to rest, take snuff, chat or readjust their loads. The safari seldom averaged more than ten miles a day and latecomers were usually dribbling into camp three or four hours after the main body. The two young Englishmen could not possibly patrol the entire safari. . . .

The young men decided that their half-wild porters would have to be put under some sort of discipline. The next day, they forced the long, straggling line to close up, and that night kept the porters in camp instead of allowing them to bivouac in a village. The result was soon forthcoming. The whole body of porters deserted the next morning leaving their loads scattered on the ground.

Grogan and Sharp started after them. They came on a small group and these Sharp stopped at the point of his revolver. Grogan kept on after the main body. Topping a little rise, he saw the deserting porters walking along below him.

Grogan called to them to come back and one of the headmen, who had been a ringleader in the trouble-making, shouted an insult. Grogan fired, knocking off the man's head covering. The other porters found the bewildered expression on the headman's face so amusing that they burst into howls of laughter and returned willingly to camp. They gave no more trouble for several weeks.

On the other side of Lake Kivu, the expedition passed a number of great volcanoes, some of them still active. Grogan, who remembered how the Watonga natives had considered him a brilliant liar when he told them of the volcanoes, pointed out the smoking cones to the four who were still with him. "What do you think now?" he asked them.

"We still think you're a great liar, Bwana," said one of the boys cheerfully.

"But there are the burning mountains in front of you," protested Grogan.

"Bwana, there is no such thing as a burning mountain," said the boy confidently. "You put those there by magic in order to fool us."

Grogan gave up.

Many of the conelike peaks had never before been seen by white men. Grogan and Sharp mapped the district and named several of the unknown mountains. One of them was named Mount Watt by Grogan, in honor, needless to say, of the pretty young girl in New Zealand who had played so prominent a part in launching the expedition.

The natives here were very friendly. There was only one case of theft. The man had greased himself, thinking that even if he were caught, no one could hold him. But Grogan tackled him around the legs and turned him over to the local chief. The next day, the safari passed the thief's head impaled on a sharp stake planted beside the trail as a warning to others. In that district, thieves were not encouraged.

Each tribe the expedition encountered had its own customs and the dietary taboos were constantly changing. In one district, the natives were astonished when the white strangers refused to eat snakes. In another, the tribesmen were surprised and disgusted when Grogan and Sharp tried to buy eggs to eat. Although this tribe had plenty of chickens, they never ate the eggs. Finally one old man brought them a basket of eggs but the eggs contained live baby chickens. When the young Englishmen refused to eat them, the angry native said, "I knew you people didn't really eat eggs. You were just trying to make a fool of me." In another area, the people refused to eat fish, considering them a kind of reptile. In still another, the natives, although desperate for meat, were revolted when Grogan suggested that they eat an elephant he had shot. "Couldn't you shoot us hippo?" They asked. "No one eats elephant meat."

In spite of illness, porter troubles and geographical obstacles, the safari continued to push on, making fairly good time. Then the party reached the borders of Mushari, between Lake Kivu and Lake Albert Edward. Here they came to a halt.

Between them and the Mushari district lay several miles of old lava beds—black, rocky, sharp-pointed rivers of stone that formed a serious barrier to the barefooted porters. But the lava beds were little more than a detail. The local natives assured the young men that a nomadic, cannibal tribe had swept into Mushari from the Congo and was laying the whole country waste. Grogan and Sharp were not fools. They had no desire to walk into the center of a district torn by native wars. So they spent several weeks trying to find some way to go around the area. On their first attempt, their native guide deserted them in a forest of impenetrable bamboo. They were miles from water and had a hard time making their way back to camp. They made a second attempt with another guide. He also deserted them, having first taken them to the top of a particularly unpleasant mountain. At this point, Grogan lost his temper.

He decided to go directly over the lava beds and so through Mushari. "I didn't believe that there were any cannibals there and if there were, I no longer cared," he admits. "I was sick of listening to native lies and native deceits. I was told that it was impossible to cross the beds. I was told there was no water there and we would all die of thirst. I was told that the country was full of savage lions. Then all our porters claimed that they were sick. They hobbled around with sticks, swearing they were too weak to walk. Fortunately, they had made themselves so unpopular with the local natives that they didn't dare be left behind and as soon as they saw we were determined to push on, they started making sandals for the trip over the lava and collecting water skins."

It was decided that Grogan would go on with a small force and Sharp would follow later with the heavier equipment and a small flock of goats which were needed as food, there being no game in the district and no way of preserving meat in the intense heat.

So at dawn one morning Grogan started out with his little force across the supposedly impassable lava beds. "It was very much like crossing the Aiguille-du-Dru glacier in Europe, with blocks of stone instead of blocks of ice," he told me. By late afternoon, they had crossed the beds and reached the fertile country on the other side. They camped that night by a little pool of clear water, delighted at having so easily surmounted the barrier.

The next morning, Grogan was astonished to see men and women who had been living in holes among the lava rocks like wild animals, come crawling out to beg for food. These wretched people told him that a few weeks before the Bareka, a cannibal tribe, had invaded the country and were killing and eating everyone they could catch. "At night, we steal down to our grain fields and try to grab a few armfuls of the unripened grain," a shivering woman told him. "But the Bareka are watching the fields and each time they catch some of us."

Grogan fed the poor creatures, but he privately thought they were probably the victims of one of the innumerable tribal wars which were so common as hardly to cause comment. Like most Europeans, he regarded cannibalism as something of a myth. He managed to persuade one of the men to act as a guide across the district and started on.

The little party now passed through some of the most beautiful country of the entire journey. On the horizon, a line of great volcanoes stood out against the sky like a Japanese painting. They walked along a well-defined path leading through green, rolling country, dotted here and there with groups of little grass huts squatting under stately trees. The emerald green of the banana plantations contrasted with the gold of the ripening grain fields, and in the distance lay vast rolls of purple hills.

As they neared the first of the grain fields, Grogan could hardly believe his eyes. Along the edges were scattered the remains of the natives who had been caught the night before by the cannibals. Cooking fires were still smoldering beside congealing pools of fresh blood. In a daze, the little party kept on. Every few yards they passed a spot where trampled grass, a few torn bits of clothing, white bones and the black ashes of a fire showed where one of the unhappy villagers had been captured. . . .

As Grogan and his men topped a little rise, they were silhouetted against the sky for a few, brief moments. Instantly they were seen by a group of the Bareka who were camped in one of the captured villages. The cannibals had not expected anyone to walk into the area in broad daylight and so had kept no watch. But after one astonished look, they leaped to their feet, grabbing up their spears and shields, and charged Grogan's party howling like wolves.

"What are they saying?" Grogan asked his guide.

"They say that they're going to kill and eat us," said the anxious guide.

"Indeed?" said Grogan. He unslung his sporting rifle from his shoulder and kneeling beside a clump of grass took steady aim. When the oncoming Bareka were within comfortable range, Grogan dropped the leader. The cannibals simply shouted the louder and came on. They knew about firearms and had expected to lose one man. But the firearms they had encountered hitherto were the muzzle-loading muskets of Arab traders. Grogan fired again and another Bareka fell. Now the yells grew less confident but still the raiders did not stop. Grogan dropped four more men in rapid succession. At last the Bareka broke and ran for cover, terrified by this strange new weapon that apparently never ran out of ammunition. . . .

Grogan's party finally managed to win clear of the cannibal area and camped for several days until Sharp, who had come by a different route, managed to catch up to them with the main safari. Reunited, the two young men worked their way north along the shores of Lake Albert Edward to Uganda. Here they separated permanently. Sharp decided to go east, crossing what is today Kenya, and take ship at Mombasa for England. Grogan continued northward, following the course of the Nile toward Egypt.

Grogan was now completely on his own and it is hard to understand how he ever managed to get through those terrible miles of swamp and desert. He lived with fever. He was almost never free from the weakening effects of dysentery. In one place, the only additional porters he could find were an old dervish prisoner with a broken leg, a small boy and a criminal lunatic in chains. A few days later, while Grogan was away trying to shoot some food, the lunatic called in the local natives and carefully distributed all Grogan's equipment among them. Then he deserted. The honest natives waited until Grogan got back and returned his belongings to him. Grogan hired canoes and tried to go north by water, but the Nile was so blocked by masses of floating water plants called "sudd" that he had to abandon this plan. He spent one night with the Baris, a people who had been driven out of their country by the warlike Dinkas and lived on islands in the river made of the compressed sudd. . . . All through this district, the mosquitoes were a constant nightmare. One of his porters who fell sick and could not drive them off was literally killed by them during the night. Once Grogan was driven to firing the dry reeds and he and his porters sat in the smoke to obtain a few hours relief from the insects.

During this part of the trip, Grogan had serious trouble with the natives only once. While passing through the Dinka territory, his group was surrounded by over a hundred of these giant people. The Dinkas averaged over six and a half feet and were stark naked. They wore their hair in a tuft, somewhat like the crest on a dragoon's helmet, which added to their height. At first these strange people seemed friendly. They crowded around the terrified porters, fingering their loads and trying to talk to them. All might have gone well if the porters had not lost their heads and bolted. Instantly the Dinkas attacked them, much as a dog will snap at anything running from it. One of the porters was speared. Two more went down under the Dinkas' clubs. Grogan was carrying a double-barreled rifle. He shot the Dinka chief and another man. At the same instant, he was attacked by a giant Dinka swinging a club. Grogan took the blow on his arm and jammed the empty gun into the man's belly. The Dinka staggered back, giving Grogan a chance to reload. He shot the man and then fired into the thick of the yelling crowd. They sullenly drew back, leaving one of the porters dying and three more insensible from club wounds.

"I never expected to see England again," Grogan admits. However, he managed to get his hysterical porters together and went on, the Dinkas following. Once, Grogan stopped and shot two more of them. The rest withdrew to a safer distance but still continued to follow.

"Camp that night was hardly a cheerful place," Grogan said. "Exhausted as we were, we still had to post sentries. I had a bad cold and my arm was so stiff from the club blow that I could hardly use it. My cook was crippled with dysentery, one of my porters had an infected foot which almost prevented him from walking, and two of the porters who had been clubbed were delirious. We could not make a fire as there was no fuel in the area. I found that my last two tins of tobacco had gone moldy so I could not even enjoy a smoke. The mosquitoes were so thick that they took turns sitting on my empty pipe, waiting for a chance to bite me."

The next morning, they went on. One of the porters who lagged behind vanished and was never seen again. Day after day the little party struggled north, sometimes through swamps where they waded in mud up to their chests and sometimes across stretches of waterless desert. All the porters were sick. They had to be prodded along at the point of a spear to keep them from lying down and dying. There was no sign of game and the last of the grain that the porters were carrying had given out. Grogan computed that in another four days' travel, he should reach the Sobat River where there should be hippo and possibly waterbirds. But could they last four more days? Grogan seriously doubted it.

Then, while plodding across the desert, Grogan saw ahead of him a long, thin stick swaying in the wind. It did not look like a tree. It was too tall for a reed. Hardly daring to believe the truth, Grogan realized it was the mast of a small boat. He had reached the Sobat. A few minutes later he met Captain Dunn, the owner of the boat.

From the Sobat, Grogan and his men went on by boat to Cairo. The news of his amazing feat had preceded him and in Cairo the young man went from dinner to dinner and from reception to reception. The four Watonga porters, who had stayed with Grogan all through the long trip from Nyasaland, were interested but not unduly impressed by the wonders of civilization. One day Grogan was out with his gunbearer when they saw a train speeding across the desert toward them. The gunbearer tapped Grogan on the shoulder, pointed to the oncoming train, and then casually handed him his elephant gun.

Grogan returned to New Zealand where he and Miss Watt were married. They traveled extensively in Europe and the United States, but like many another man, Grogan could not get Africa out of his blood. When the Boer War came, he promptly enlisted as a captain in the Fourth Royal Munster Fusiliers. An attack of malaria laid him low, and he was hospitalized next to another young man who was planning to go to Kenya after the war and start a timber concern. The two men formed a partnership and at the end of hostilities, traveled to Nairobi, then a city of tents. Here Mrs. Grogan joined her husband.

The young colony was racked by many troubles, not the least of them being the problem of administering an area three times the size of the British Isles with a force of a few hundred white men. Grogan threw himself enthusiastically into politics. His methods hardly endeared him to the government, but they were effective. At one period, a defect in the mining laws allowed a man to stake out a claim anywhere in the colony. Irresponsible men were laying out mining claims across the intended routes of main highways and valuable farming lands. After vainly pleading with the government to have the law altered, Grogan went out one evening and gravely pegged out a claim all around Nairobi. A special meeting of the alarmed council had to be called in the middle of the night to change the law as Grogan was threatening to start tearing up the main street with a pickax.

Grogan left Kenya to take part in the First World War

during which he received his colonelcy and a D.S.O. In World War II, he acted as the West Coast liaison officer for the British forces. In his later years, the colonel decided to take up farming. He and Mrs. Grogan settled at Taveta, not far from the Tanganyika border. By an ingenious system of irrigation canals, he tapped the melting snows of Kilimanjaro and turned what was once one of the most barren and desolate stretches of bush country in all Kenya into one of the most prosperous farms.

There were many young men like Colonel Grogan in the England of fifty years ago. Today, I fear that they are a vanishing breed. The world is the poorer for their passing.

AQUALUNG DIVING

(From THE SILENT WORLD. New York: Harper & Brothers, 1953)

Capt. Jacques-Yves Cousteau founded the French Navy's Undersea Research Group in 1945, but he began goggle-diving and spear fishing in the Mediterranean in the nineteen-thirties. He developed the aqualung diving apparatus, which has made underwater activities so popular.
The following extract describes the first aqualung dive. I have also taken a short extract on sound in the sea and the flora and fauna to be found at varying depths.

One morning in June, 1943, I went to the railway station at Bandol on the French Riviera and received a wooden case expressed from Paris. In it was a new and promising device, the result of years of struggle and dreams, an automatic compressed-air diving lung conceived by Émile Gagnan and myself. I rushed it to Villa Barry where my diving comrades, Philippe Tailliez and Frédéric Dumas waited. No children ever opened a Christmas present with more excitement than ours when we unpacked the first "aqualung." If it worked, diving could be revolutionized.

We found an assembly of three moderate-sized cylinders of compressed air, linked to an air regulator the size of an alarm clock. From the regulator there extended two tubes, joining on a mouthpiece. With this equipment harnessed to the back, a watertight glass mask over the eyes and nose, and rubber foot fins, we intended to make unencumbered flights in the depths of the sea.

We hurried to a sheltered cove which would conceal our activity from curious bathers and Italian occupation troops. I checked the air pressure. The bottles contained air condensed to one hundred and fifty times atmospheric pressure. It was difficult to contain my excitement and discuss calmly the plan of the first dive. Dumas, the best goggle diver in France, would stay on shore keeping warm and rested, ready to dive to my aid, if necessary. My wife, Simone, would swim out on the surface with a schnorkel breathing tube and watch me through her submerged mask. If she signaled anything had gone wrong, Dumas could dive to me in seconds. "Didi," as he was known on the Riviera, could skin dive to sixty feet.

My friends harnessed the three-cylinder block on my back with the regulator riding at the nape of my neck and the hoses looped over my head. I spat on the inside of my shatterproof glass mask and rinsed it in the surf, so that mist would not form inside. I molded the soft rubber flanges of the mask tightly over forehead and cheekbones. I fitted the mouthpiece under my lips and gripped the nodules between my teeth. A vent the size of a paper clip was to pass my inhalations and exhalations beneath the sea. Staggering under the fifty-pound apparatus, I walked with a Charlie Chaplin waddle into the sea.

The diving lung was designed to be slightly buoyant. I reclined in the chilly water to estimate my compliance with Archimedes' principle that a solid body immersed in liquid is buoyed up by a force equal to the weight of the liquid displaced. Dumas justified me with Archimedes by attaching seven pounds of lead to my belt. I sank gently to the sand. I breathed sweet effortless air. There was a faint whistle when I inhaled and a light rippling sound of bubbles when I breathed out. The regulator was adjusting pressure precisely to my needs.

I looked into the sea with the same sense of trespass that I have felt on every dive. A modest canyon opened below, full of dark green weeds, black sea urchins and small flower-like white algae. Fingerlings browsed in the scene. The sand sloped down into a clear blue infinity. The sun struck so brightly I had to squint. My arms hanging at my sides, I kicked the fins languidly and traveled down, gaining speed, watching the beach reeling past. I stopped kicking and the momentum carried me on a fabulous glide. When I stopped, I slowly emptied my lungs and held my breath. The diminished volume of my body decreased the lifting force of water, and I sank dreamily down. I inhaled a great chestful and retained it. I rose toward the surface.

My human lungs had a new role to play, that of a sensitive ballasting system. I took normal breaths in a slow rhythm, bowed my head and swam smoothly down to thirty feet. I felt no increasing water pressure, which at that depth is twice that of the surface. The aqualung automatically fed me increased compressed air to meet the new pressure layer. Through the fragile human lung linings this counter-pressure was being transmitted to the bloodstream and instantly spread throughout the incompressible body. My brain received no subjective news of the pressure. I was at ease, except for a pain in the middle ear and sinus cavities. I swallowed as one does in a landing airplane to open my Eustachian tubes and healed the pain (I did not wear ear plugs, a dangerous practice when under water. Ear plugs would have trapped a pocket of air between them and the eardrums. Pressure building up in the Eustachian tubes would have forced my eardrums outward, eventually to the bursting point.)

I reached the bottom in a state of transport. A school of silvery sars (goat bream), round and flat as saucers, swam in a rocky chaos. I looked up and saw the surface shining like a defective mirror. In the center of the looking glass was the trim silhouette of Simone, reduced to a doll. I waved. The doll waved at me.

I became fascinated with my exhalations. The bubbles swelled on the way up through lighter pressure layers, but were peculiarly flattened like mushroom caps by their eager push against the medium. I conceived the importance bubbles were to have for us in the dives to come. As long as air boiled on the surface all was well below. If the bubbles disappeared there would be anxiety, emergency measures, despair. They roared out of the regulator and kept me company. I felt less alone.

I swam across the rocks and compared myself favorably with the sars. To swim fishlike, horizontally, was the logical method in a medium eight hundred times denser than air. To halt and hang attached to nothing, no lines or air pipe to the surface, was a dream. At night I had often had visions of flying by extending my arms as wings. Now I flew without wings. (Since that first aqualung flight, I have never had a dream of flying.)

I thought of the helmet diver arriving where I was on his ponderous boots and struggling to walk a few yards, obsessed with his umbilici and his head imprisoned in copper. On skin dives I had seen him leaning dangerously forward to make a step, clamped in heavier pressure at the ankles than the head, a cripple in an alien land. From this day forward we would swim across miles of country no man had known, free and level, with our flesh feeling what the fish scales know.

I experimented with all possible maneuvers of the aqualung—loops, somersaults, and barrel rolls. I stood upside down on one finger and burst out laughing, a shrill distorted laugh. Nothing I did altered the automatic rhythm of air. Delivered from gravity and buoyancy I flew around in space.

I could attain almost two knots' speed, without using my arms. I soared vertically and passed my own bubbles. I went down to sixty feet. We had been there many times without breathing aids, but we did not know what happened below

that boundary. How far could we go with this strange device?
. . . . Our new key to the hidden world promised wonders.

The sea is a most silent world. I say this deliberately on
long accumulated evidence and aware that wide publicity
has recently been made on the noises of the sea. Hydrophones
have recorded clamors that have been sold as phonographic
curiosa, but the recordings have been grossly amplified. It
is not the reality of the sea as we have known it with naked
ears. There are noises under water, very interesting ones that
the sea transmits exceptionally well, but a diver does not hear
boiler factories.

An undersea sound is so rare that one attaches great importance to it. The creatures of the sea express fear, pain and
joy without audible comment. The old round of life and
death passes silently, save among the mammals—whales and
porpoises. The sea is unaffected by man's occasional uproars
of dynamite and ships' engines. It is a silent jungle, in which
the diver's sounds are keenly heard—the soft roar of exhalations, the lisp of incoming air and the hoots of a comrade.
One's hunting companion may be hundreds of yards away
out of sight, but his missed harpoons may be clearly heard
clanging on the rocks, and when he returns one may taunt
him by holding up a finger for each shot he missed.

Attentive ears may occasionally perceive a remote creaking sound, especially if the breath is held for a moment. The
hydrophone can, of course, swell this faint sound to a din,
helpful for analysis, but not the way it sounds to the submerged ear. We have not been able to adduce a theory to ex-
plain the creaking sounds. Syrian fishermen select fishing
grounds by putting their heads down into their boats to the
focal point of the sound shell that is formed by the hull.
Where they hear creaking sounds they cast nets. They believe that the sound somehow emanates from rocks below,
and rocks mean fish pasturage. Some marine biologists sup-

pose the creaking sound comes from thick thousands of tiny shrimps, scraping pincers in concert. Such a shrimp in a specimen jar will transmit audible snaps. But the Syrians net fish, not shrimps. When we have dived into creaking areas we have never found a single shrimp. The distant rustle seems stronger in calm seas after a storm, but this is not always the case. The more we experience the sea, the less certain we are of conclusions.

Some fish can croak like frogs. At Dakar I swam in a loud orchestration of these monotonous animals. Whales, porpoises, croakers and whatever makes the creaking noise are the only exceptions we know to the silence of the sea.

Some fish have internal ears with otoliths, or ear stones, which make attractive necklaces called "lucky stones." But fish show little or no reaction to noises. The evidence is that they are much more responsive to nonaudible vibrations. They have a sensitive lateral line along their flanks which is, in effect, the organ of a sixth sense. As a fish undulates, the lateral receiver probably establishes its main sense of being. We think the lateral line can detect pressure waves, such as those generated by a struggling creature at a great distance. We have noticed that hooting at fish does not perturb them, but pressure waves generated by rubber foot fins seem to have a distinct influence. To approach fish we move our legs in a liquid sluggish stroke, expressing a peaceful intention. A nervous or rapid kick will empty the area of fish, even those behind rocks which cannot see us. The alarm spreads in successive explosions; one small fleeing creature is enough to panic the others. The water trembles with emergency and fish far from sight receive the silent warning.

It has become second nature to swim unobtrusively among them. We will pass casually through a landscape where all sorts of fish are placidly enjoying life and showing us the full measure of acceptance. Then, without an untoward move on our part, the area will be deserted of all fish. What portent removes hundreds of creatures, silently and at once? Were porpoises beating up pressure waves out of sight, or were hungry dentex marauding off in the mists? All we know, hanging in the abandoned space, is that an unhearable raid siren has sent all but us to shelter. We feel like deaf men. With all senses attuned to the sea, we are still without the sixth sense, perhaps the most important of all in undersea existence.

At Dakar I was diving in water where sharks ranged peacefully among hundreds of tempting red porgies, unwary of the predators. I returned to the boat and threw in a fishing line and hooked several porgies. The sharks snapped them in two before I could boat them. I think perhaps the struggle of the hooked fish transmitted vibrations that told the sharks there was easy prey available, animals in distress. In tropical waters we have used dynamite to rally sharks. I doubt whether the explosion is anything more than a dull, insignificant noise to them, but they answer the pressure waves of the fluttering fish that have been injured near the burst.

On the Azure Coast there are vertical reefs two hundred feet deep. Going straight down one of these walls is an unusual excursion into the variety of the sea and its abrupt changes of environment. Mountain climbers, like our friend, Marcel Ichac, who have gone down the reefs with us, are surprised at the changes. Going up a mountain one struggles through miles of foothills, through extended zones of trees to the snow-line, to the tree-line, and into the thin air. On the reef the changes are rapid, almost bewildering, from one zone to another. The top ten fathoms, lighted by sunny lace from the surface, are populated with nervous darting fish. Then one enters a strange country upon which dusk has fallen at noon, an autumnal clime with insalubrious air that makes the head heavy, like that of a person doomed to live in a smoggy industrial town.

Gliding down the rock façade one looks back at the world where summer shines. Then one comes to the cold layer and grows tense for the leap into winter. Inside the dull dark cold one forgets the sun. One forgets a lot. The ears no longer announce pressure changes and the air tastes like pennies. An introspective calm rules there. The green mossy rocks are replaced by Gothic stones, pierced, cusped and enfinialed. Each vault and arcade of the bottom rocks is a little world with a sandy beach and a tableau of fish.

Deeper down are miniature blue trees with white blossoms. These are the real coral, the semi-precious *corallium rubrum* in brittle limestone fantasies of form. For centuries coral was commercially dredged in the Mediterranean with "coral crosses," a type of wooden drag that smashed down the trees and recovered a few branches. The once-thick trees on the floor that may have taken hundreds of years to grow, are no more. The surviving coral grows below twenty fathoms in protected recesses and grottoes, accumulating from the ceiling like stalactites. It may be gathered only by divers.

A diver entering a coral cave must be aware of its appearance in the sea's deceiving color filter. The coral branches appear blue-black. They are covered with pale blossoms that retract and disappear when disturbed. Red coral is out of fashion at the moment and sells for about ten dollars a pound.

In the zone of red coral black-striped lobster horns protrude from the lacunae of the reef. When a diver's hand comes near, the lobster stirs with a dry grating sound. On the rocks are living tumors and growths resembling udders, long fleshy threads, chalice-shaped formations, and forms like mushrooms. Objects may no longer be distinguished by color, although there are supernatural colors to them—the violet of wine dregs, blue-blacks, yellowish-greens; all muted and grayed, but somehow vibrant.

Now at the base of the reef, the sand begins, bare and monotonously receding into the floor. There, on the border of life, nothing grows or crawls. One moves automatically without brain directives. In the recesses of the brain, one revives an old notion—return to the surface. The drugged state disappears on the rise along the wall, the departure from a discolored land, a country that has never shown its real face.

Fish do not like to go up or down, but swim on a chosen level of the reef, like tenants of a certain floor of a skyscraper. The ground-floor occupants, wrasses, groupers and Spanish bream, rarely venture to upper stories of the cliff dwelling. The dentex pace back and forth just above the sandy fields. The sars pass in and out of the rocks with a busy and determined air. The wrasses are slow and seem bored. The Spanish bream are slower still. They hang against the cliff sucking the rocks like lollipops. Higher and away from the reef tower, the pelagic fish roam, but they too seem to prefer a given stratum and rarely swim up or down. Fish do not like the effort of making pressure changes.

Fish seem to glide forever as long as one does not startle them. What do fish do all day long? Most of the time they swim. We have rarely witnessed fish feeding. The sar is sometimes found along a rock, browsing with its goatish teeth on clinging sea urchins. It methodically clips away the urchin's brittle spines, spits them out, and chews down until it is able to cut open the carapace and reach the meal inside. *Rouquiers** eat all the time. They gobble invisible tidbits from the soil, or stand vertically, blowing small dust clouds and swallowing them. The fussy mullet rustles across the rocks, sucking weeds with its thick white lips, cleaning off the fish eggs and spores. Sea bream graze by the hundreds on the ocean prairies. When our presence disturbs them they relieve themselves in immense green clouds and depart.

We have waited for years to witness the meal of a carniv-

---

* There seems to be no English or American equivalent for the name of this fish.

orous bass, dentex, conger or moray, and have never seen it. We know only from surface observation that the predators have two strict daily mealtimes, in the morning and evening, as regularly observed as a boarding-school dinner gong. The vast shoals of sprats, sardines, or needlefish, living near the surface, are savagely attacked from below. The sea boils and the air flickers with the hail of little bodies, leaping out and falling back. Sea birds join the massacre from the other side of the barrier, diving and flaunting the sparkling prey in their bills. When we dive in the banquet stops. We see the big ones roving below, waiting for us to leave. The small ones find a moment of surcease near the surface. Fish will not feed near divers. The war for food lasts a half hour, then a truce comes and eaters and those to be eaten tomorrow mingle sociably again in the quiet flood.

Eagerly as we have sought to observe carnivorous feeding, so have we awaited almost as vainly for the mating drama. Mullets are the most shameless. They breed in September in the warm shore waters of the Mediterranean. The females stroll up and down with composure while the excited males flutter around, rubbing themselves feverishly against their mates. At that season the majestic Spanish bream forget their lonely arrogance and aggregate in incredible swarms, pressed so closely against each other there is scarcely room to slide. No two fish hold the same position in the amorous mêlée, quite unlike the normal formations of a school.

Fish have different ways of showing their curiosity. Often while swimming along we will turn back abruptly and see the muzzles of echelons of creatures following us with avid interest. The dentex gives us a passing glance of contempt. The sea bass approaches us, investigates and swims away. The liche feigns indifference, but closes in for a better look and is quickly satisfied.

Not so with the merou. The grouper is the ocean's scholar, sincerely interested in our species. It approaches and looks at us with large, touching eyes, full of puzzlement, and stays to survey us. The merou probably attains a hundred pounds. We have speared and weighed individuals of fifty-five pounds and have seen others which seem twice that weight. The creature is a cousin of the tropical jewfish, which grows as big as five hundred pounds. The merou lives near the coast in thirty feet of clouded turbulent water, close to the rock forts it holds so stubbornly. There are a few radical merous who have taken caves further up on the shelf in ten-foot depths. They are suspicious individualists who rarely emerge, have a clear conception of danger, and grow old peering out their doors.

They are the most inquisitive animals we have found in the sea. In virgin territory merous swim out of their holes and come great distances to see us. They sit below and look up full in our faces. With their big pectorals spread like the wings of baroque angels, they stare sanctimoniously at us. When we move they shake themselves, and leap to new vantage points. When at last they go back home, they watch us from their doors and run to a window to see us depart.

When the tiny black pomfrets with forked tails, half the size of a goldfish, throng around the merous, the groupers stare through at us like veiled women. If we dive into the screen of pomfrets, it breaks like a window glass and the merou vanishes. A hundred feet down the fish apparently do not associate us with the surface. In the sad bluish gloom one is accepted in the jungle and its inhabitants have no fear, merely curiosity toward the extraordinary animal with a mania for spreading bubbles.

The merou eats everything in the path of its huge open mouth. In go octopi and the stones they may be clinging to, whole cuttlefish in their shells, thorny sea spiders, lobsters and entire fish. If the merou accidentally swallows a fishing hook, it usually severs the line. One of Dumas's merous had two fish hooks in its stomach, the metal encysted with age.

The merou has a chameleon's talent. Mostly they are reddish brown. They can put on a marbleized pattern or dark stripes. Once we found a white one flat on the sand. We thought it was the pallor of death and decay, but the ghost stirred up, turned brown, and made off.

One morning we were swimming across a large fissure fourteen fathoms down. We halted and lay in the water, looking down at a group of twenty to thirty-pound adolescent merous. They swam straight up toward us and then turned over and glided down like children on a slide. Below them were a dozen larger individuals moving in a preoccupied figure. One of the merous turned white. The others paraded by it closely. One stopped beside the albino and itself turned white. Then both uncolored animals rubbed themselves slowly against each other, perhaps in an act of love. We stared, unable to comprehend the sight. What was the ceremony in the dim rocks? It was as strange as the elephant dance that little Toomai saw.

The merou has a special and old familiar place in our undersea experience. We feel sure that we could tame one, by training that generous curiosity toward becoming a pet.

THE LOST MINES OF MURIBECA

(From LOST TRAILS, LOST CITIES. New York: Funk & Wagnalls Co., 1953)

Colonel Fawcett disappeared in 1925 on an expedition which he was sure was to be his last, as he was convinced that this time he would find the lost cities of the Incas for which he had searched from 1906 to 1925. This great explorer was sure that the Inca civilization still existed and that the Incas' descendants would be found living in the cities and carrying on the old traditions. Although many expeditions were formed to look for him, no trace has so far been found and it seems unlikely that we shall ever know what happened to him, his son Jack and his son's friend Raleigh Rimmel. The entire expedition disappeared. Here is one of the stories he tells in his book, one of the stories that convinced him that his search would end with a great discovery, and his last message.

When Diego Alvarez struggled landwards through the Atlantic swell in a welter of wreckage from the disintegrating caravel, it was to land, exhausted, on a shore absolutely unknown to this sixteenth-century Portuguese. Only twenty-four years previously Columbus had discovered the New World and fired the imaginations of Iberian adventurers.

Here, on the coast of Brazil where Bahia now stands, anything might exist. Behind the forest's edge on top of those cliffs were surely to be found wonderful things, and he—Diego Alvarez—would be the first of his race to set eyes on them.

The place where he came ashore, sole survivor from the wreck, was in the territory of the cannibal Tupinambas. Perhaps he escaped being eaten by reason of his strangeness; perhaps his captors considered it a triumph over neighbouring tribes to display their captive alive. For his salvation the Portuguese had principally to thank an Indian girl named Paraguaçu, the Pocahontas of South America, who took a fancy to him and became his wife.

For many years the Portuguese mariner lived with the Indians. A number of his countrymen came to Brazil, and he was able to establish friendly relations between them and the savages. Finally he managed to bring Paraguaçu into the fold of the Church, and a sister of hers married another Portuguese adventurer. The child of her sister's marriage, Melchior Dias Moreyra, spent most of his life with the Indians, and was known by them as Muribeca. He discovered many mines, and accumulated vast quantities of silver, gold, and precious stones, which were worked by the skilful Tapuya tribes into so wonderful a treasure that the early European colonists were filled with envy.

Muribeca had a son called Roberio Dias, who as a lad was familiar with the mines where his father's vast wealth originated. About 1610 Roberio Dias approached the Portuguese King, Dom Pedro II, with an offer to hand over the mines in exchange for the title of Marquis das Minas. He showed a rich specimen of silver-bearing ore and temptingly promised more silver than there was iron at Bilbao. He was only partly believed, but the royal greed for treasure was strong enough to cause a patent to be drawn up for the marquisate.

If Roberio Dias thought he would leave the court a marquis he was mistaken. Old Dom Pedro II was too cunning for that. The patent was sealed and delivered to a commission entrusted to hand it over only after the mines had been disclosed. But Dias in his turn had suspicions. He was not one to trust blindly to the King's faith. While the expedition was some distance from Bahia he managed to persuade the of-

ficer in command of the Commission to open the envelope
and allow him to see the patent. He found that he was down
for a military commission as captain, and no more—not a
word about the marquisate! That settled it. Dias refused to
hand over the mines, so the enraged officer took him back by
force to Bahia, where he was flung into prison. Here he remained for two years, and then he was allowed to buy his
freedom for 9,000 crowns. In 1622 he died, and the secret of
the mines was never disclosed.

The secret of the mines was lost, but for years expeditions
scoured the country in an effort to locate them. As failure
succeeded failure, belief in their existence died away to survive only as myth, yet there were always some hardy souls
ready to brave hostile savages and slow starvation for the
chance of discovering a New Potosí.

If you are romantically minded—and most of us are, I
think—you have in the foregoing the background for a story
so fascinating that I know none to compare. I myself came
upon it in an old document still preserved at Rio de Janeiro,
and, in the light of evidence gleaned from many quarters,
believe it implicitly. I am not going to offer a literal trans-
lation of the strange account given in the document—the
crabbed Portuguese script is broken in several places—but
the story begins in 1743, when a native of Minas Gerais,
whose name has not been preserved, decided to make a
search for the Lost Mines of Muribeca.

It was always difficult to take cargo animals through the
trackless hinterland. There were numerous rivers and bogs
everywhere; pasture was coarse, and the continuous attacks
of vampire bats soon finished the animals off. Climate ranged
from very cold to extreme heat, and total drought would be
followed by days of sheer deluge, so that a fair amount of
equipment had to be carried. Yet Raposo and his band gave
little consideration to such drawbacks, and set out hopefully
into the wilds.

Exactly where they went I have only lately discovered. It was roughly northwards. There were no maps of the country in those days, and no member of the party knew anything about land navigation, so the clues in the record they left are entirely unreliable. Indians accompanied them from point to point and suggested the routes taken, otherwise they merely wandered into the unknown and left it to fortune to bring them to the coveted objective.

The time came when the party was travelling eastward again, towards the coast settlements, tired of this seemingly endless wandering, and disheartened by their failure to locate the lost mines. Raposo was almost ready to believe them a myth, and his companions had long ago decided that no such mines existed. They had come through swamps and bush country when jagged mountains showed up ahead, beyond a grassy plain broken by thin belts of green forest. Raposo in his narrative describes them poetically, "They seemed to reach the ethereal regions and to serve as a throne for the wind and the stars themselves."

These were no ordinary mountains. As the party came nearer, the sides lit up in flame, for it had been raining and the setting sun was reflected from wet rocks rich in crystals and that slightly opaque quartz which is so common in this part of Brazil. To the eager explorers they seemed to be studded with gems. Streams leaped from rock to rock, and over the crest of the ridge a rainbow formed, as though to hint that treasure was to be found at its feet.

"An omen!" cried Raposo. "See! We have found the treasure house of the great Muribeca!"

Night came down and forced them to camp before reaching the foot of those wonderful mountains; and next morning, when the sun came up from behind them, the crags appeared black and menacing.

To the eyes of Raposo and his comrades their height was vast, and when they reached them it was to find sheer, unscalable precipices. All day they struggled over boulders and crevices, seeking a way up those glassy sides. Rattlesnakes abounded—and there is no remedy for the bite of the Brazilian species. Wearied by the hard going and constant vigilance to avoid these snakes, Raposo called a halt.

"Three leagues we have come and still no way up," he said. "It would be better to return to our old trail and find a way northwards. What do you say?"

"Camp!" was the reply. "Let's camp. We've had enough for one day. Tomorrow we can return."

"Very well," answered the leader; and then to two of the men, "You, José and Manoel—off you go to find wood for the fire!"

Camp was pitched and the party was resting when confused shouting and a crashing in the bush brought them to their feet, guns in hand. José and Manoel burst into view.

"*Patrão, Patrão!*" they cried. "We've found it—the way up!"

Searching for firewood in the low scrub they had seen a dead tree at the edge of a small wooded creek. This was the best fuel to be had, and they were making their way towards it when a deer sprang up on the other side of the creek and disappeared beyond a corner of the cliff. Unslinging their guns the two men followed as quickly as they could, for here was meat enough to last them several days.

The animal had vanished, but beyond the outcropping of rock they came on a deep cleft in the face of the precipice, and saw that it was possible to climb up through it to the summit. Deer and firewood were forgotten in the excitement.

They broke camp at once, shouldered their packs, and set off with Manoel leading. With ejaculations of wonder they entered the crevice in single file, to find that it widened somewhat inside. It was rough going, but here and there were traces of what looked like old paving, and in places the sheer walls of the cleft seemed to bear the almost obliterated marks of tools.

The climb was so difficult that three hours passed before

they emerged torn and breathless on a ledge high above the surrounding plain. From here to the ridge was clear ground, and soon they were standing shoulder to shoulder at the top, gazing, dumb with amazement, at the view spread out below them.

There at their feet, about four miles away, was a huge city.

Immediately they flung themselves down and edged back behind the cover of the rocks, hoping that the inhabitants had not seen their distant figures against the sky, for this might be a colony of the hated Spaniards. Then again, it might be such a city as Cuzco, the ancient capital of the Incas in Peru, inhabited by a race of highly civilized people still holding out against the encroachments of the European invaders.

No fires were lit that night, and the men talked in whispers. They were awed by the sight of civilization after those long years in the wilds, and by no means confident of their safety. Two hours before nightfall Raposo had sent off two Portuguese and four Negroes to reconnoitre and find out what sort of people lived in this mysterious place. Nervously the rest of the party awaited their return, and every forest noise— every insect song and whisper of the foliage—was sinister. But the scouts had nothing to tell when they came back. Lack of cover had kept them from venturing too near the city, but no sign of occupation had they seen. The Indians of the party were as mystified as Raposo and his followers. By nature superstitious, certain parts of the country to them were "taboo," and they were filled with alarm.

Raposo, however, was able to prevail on one of the Indians to scout forward single-handed after sunrise next morning. No one had slept much during the night, and their curiosity about the Indian's fate kept them from resting in the more comfortable light of day. At midday he crept back into camp, obviously terrified, and insisting that the city was uninhabited.

Early next morning Raposo sent ahead an advance guard

of four Indians and followed towards the city with the rest of the party. As they came near the overgrown walls the Indians met them with the same story—the place was deserted—and so with less caution they followed the trail to an entrance under three arches formed of huge stone slabs. So impressive was this cyclopean structure—similar, probably, to much that can yet be seen at Sacsahuaman in Peru— that no man dared speak, but slipped by the blackened stones as stealthily as a cat.

High above the central arch characters of some sort were graven deeply into the weatherworn stone. Raposo, uneducated though he was, could see that this was no modern writing. A feeling of vast age brooded over everything, and it took a distinct effort for him to issue in a hoarse, unnatural voice the orders to advance.

The arches were still in a fair state of preservation, but one or two of the colossal uprights had twisted slightly on their bases. The men passed through and entered what had once been a wide street, but littered now with broken pillars and blocks of masonry rank with the parasitic vegetation of the tropics. On either side were two-storeyed houses built of great blocks fitting together with mortarless joints of almost incredible accuracy, the porticos, narrow above and wide below, decorated with elaborate carvings of what they took to be demons.

The description, coming from men who had never seen Cuzco and Sacsahuaman, or the other wonder cities of old Peru—which were incredibly ancient when the Incas first came upon them—cannot be lightly dismissed. What they saw and related tallies closely with much that we can still see today.

There was ruin everywhere, but many buildings were roofed with great stone slabs still in position. Those of the party who dared to enter the dark interiors and raise their voices ran out at the echoes flung back at them from walls and vaulted ceilings. It was impossible to say if any remnants of furnishings remained, for in most cases inner walls had collapsed, covering the floors with debris, and the bat droppings of centuries formed a thick carpet underfoot. So old was this place that perishables such as furniture and textiles must have disintegrated long ago.

Huddled together like a flock of frightened sheep, the men proceeded down the street and came to a vast square. Here in the centre was a huge column of black stone, and upon it the effigy, in perfect preservation, of a man with one hand on his hip and the other pointing towards the north. The majesty of this statue struck deep into the hearts of the Portuguese and they crossed themselves reverently. Carved obelisks of the same black stone, partially ruined, stood at each corner of the square, while running the length of one side was a building so magnificent in design and decoration that it must have been a palace. The walls and roof had collapsed in many places, but its great square columns were still intact. A broad flight of ruined stone steps led up and into a wide hall, where traces of colour still clung to the frescoes and carvings. Bats in countless thousands winged in circles through the dim chambers and the acrid reek of their droppings was suffocating.

The explorers were glad to get out into the clean air. The figure of a youth was carved over what seemed to be the principal doorway. It portrayed a beardless figure, naked from the waist up, with shield in hand and a band across one shoulder. The head was crowned with what looked to them like a wreath of laurel, judging by Grecian statuary they had seen in Portugal. Below were inscribed characters remarkably like those of ancient Greece. Raposo copied them on a tablet and reproduced them in his narrative.

Opposite the palace was the ruin of another huge building, evidently a temple. Eroded carvings of figures, animals and birds covered the walls that remained, and over the portal were more characters which again were copied as faithfully as Raposo or one of his followers was capable of doing.

Beyond the square and the main street the city lay in complete ruin, in some places actually buried under mounds of earth on which not a blade of grass or other vegetation grew. Here and there were gaping chasms, and when the explorers dropped rocks into these not a sound came up to indicate bottom. There was little doubt now what had devastated the place. The Portuguese knew what earthquakes were and what destruction they could do. Here whole buildings had been swallowed, leaving perhaps only a few carved blocks to show where they had stood. It was not difficult to imagine something of the awful cataclysm that had laid waste this glorious place, tumbled columns and blocks weighing perhaps fifty tons and more, and that had destroyed in a matter of minutes the painstaking labour of a thousand years!

The far side of the square terminated in a river about thirty yards wide, flowing straight and easily from the northwest and vanishing in distant forest. At one time a fine promenade had bordered on the river, but the masonry was now broken up and much had subsided into the water. On the other side of the river were fields that once were cultivated, still covered with abundant coarse grass and a carpet of flowers. Rice had propagated and thrived in the shallow swamps all about, and here the waters were alive with duck.

Deserted and ruined the city was, but its environs of rich fields provided far more food for the explorers than they could find in the virgin forest. It is therefore not surprising that in spite of their awe of the place none of the men was anxious to leave it. Their fear gave way to a lust for treasure, and this increased when João Antonio—the only member of the party to be mentioned by name in the document—found a small gold coin in the rubble. On one face it bore the effigy of a youth on his knees, and on the other a bow, a crown and a musical instrument of some sort. The place must be full of gold, they told themselves; when the inhabitants fled they would have taken only the things most necessary for their survival.

Gathering rice from the swamps and hunting duck—if hunting it could be called—were perilous. Anacondas big enough to kill a man were common; and poisonous snakes, attracted by the game, swarmed everywhere, feeding not only on the birds but also on jerboas—"rats jumping like fleas," as the narrator describes them. Wild dogs, large grey brutes as big as wolves, haunted the plains, yet not a man would sleep within the city. Camp was pitched just beyond the gate where they first entered, and from here they watched at sunset the legions of bats emerging from the great buildings to disperse in the gloaming with a dry rustling of wings like the first breath of an approaching storm. By day the sky was black with swallows, greedy for the prolific insect life.

Francisco Raposo had no idea where they were, but at last decided to follow the river through the forest, hoping that his Indians would remember the landmarks when he returned with a properly equipped expedition to comb the wealth out of these ruins. Fifty miles down they came to a mighty waterfall, and in an adjoining cliff face were found distinct signs of mine workings. Here they tarried longer. Game was plentiful, several of the men were down with fever and the Indians were nervous about the possibility of hostile tribes in the vicinity. Below the fall the river broadened out into a series of swampy lagoons, as these South American rivers have a way of doing.

Investigation proved the suspected mineshafts to be holes they had no means of exploring, but at their mouths lay scattered about a quantity of rich silver ore. Here and there were caves hewn out of the cliff by hand, some of them sealed off by great stone slabs engraved with strange glyphs. The caves might have been the tombs of the city's monarchs and high priests. The men tried in vain to move the stone slabs.

The adventurers pictured themselves as rich men and agreed to say nothing to anybody except the Viceroy, to whom Raposo owed a debt of gratitude. They would return here as soon as possible, take possession of the mines, and remove all treasure from the city.

In the meantime a scouting party had been sent out to explore farther down river. After traversing the lagoons and backwaters for nine days they caught a glimpse of a canoe paddled by two "white people" with long black hair and dressed in some sort of clothing. They fired a shot to attract attention, but the canoe made off and vanished from view. Weary of the fatiguing business of making wide detours around the swamps, and afraid to continue farther down with so small a party, they returned to the fall.

Raposo felt the need of caution now that he and his followers had fortunes within their grasp. He had no wish to risk an encounter with hostile Indians and so he struck off eastwards. After some months of hard travel they reached the bank of the São Francisco River, crossed from there to the Paraguaçu, and at length came to Bahia. From here he sent to the Viceroy, Don Luiz Peregrino de Carvalho Menezes de Athayde, the document from which this story is taken.

Here is the last message from my father, dated May 29, 1925, and sent back with the *peons*. After this not another thing was heard from them, and to this day their fate has remained a mystery.

"The attempt to write is fraught with much difficulty owing to the legions of flies that pester one from dawn till dark— and sometimes all through the night! The worst are the tiny ones smaller than a pinhead, almost invisible but stinging like a mosquito. Clouds of them are always present. Millions

of bees add to the plague, and other bugs galore. The stinging horrors get all over one's hands, and madden. Even the
head nets won't keep them out. As for mosquito nets, the
pests fly through them!

"We hope to get through this region in a few days, and
are camped here for a couple of days to arrange for the return of the *peons*, who are anxious to get back, having had
enough of it—and I don't blame them. We go on with eight
animals—three saddle mules, four cargo mules, and a *mad-
rinha*, a leading animal which keeps the others together.
Jack is well and fit, getting stronger every day even though
he suffers a bit from the insects. I myself am bitten or stung
by ticks, and these *piums*, as they call the tiny ones, all over
the body. Raleigh I am anxious about. He still has one leg
in a bandage, but won't go back. So far we have plenty of
food, and no need to walk, but I am not sure how long this
will last. There may be so little for the animals to eat. I cannot hope to stand up to this journey better than Jack or
Raleigh, but I had to do it. Years tell, in spite of the spirit
of enthusiasm.

"I calculate to contact the Indians in about a week or ten
days, when we should be able to reach the waterfall so
much talked about.

"Here we are at Dead Horse Camp, Lat. 11° 43′ S. and
54° 35′ W., the spot where my horse died in 1920. Only his
white bones remain. We can bathe ourselves here, but the
insects make it a matter of great haste. Nevertheless, the
season is good. It is *very cold* at night, and fresh in the morning; but insects and heat come by midday, and from then
till six o'clock in the evening it is sheer misery in camp.

"You need have no fear of any failure. . . ."

Those last words he wrote to my mother come to me like
an echo across the twenty-six years elapsed since then.

"You need have no fear of any failure. . . ."

CHARLES A. LINDBERGH

NEW YORK TO PARIS

(From WE. New York: G. P. Putnam's Sons, 1927)

On May 20-21, 1927, Captain Charles A. Lindbergh, a young airmail pilot from Minnesota, won worldwide fame literally overnight by becoming the first man to fly an airplane non-stop between the American and European continents. His plane, the Spirit of St. Louis, *was a Ryan single-engine monoplane built especially for Lindbergh's pioneer transatlantic attempt. Taking off from Roosevelt Field, Long Island, New York, early in the morning of May 20th, Captain Lindbergh landed safely at Le Bourget airport, Paris, late in the evening of the following day. In the following excerpt he describes this historic flight, which ushered in a new era of transoceanic air transportation.*

At New York we checked over the plane, engine and instruments, which required several short flights over the field.

When the plane was completely inspected and ready for the trans-Atlantic flight, there were dense fogs reported along the coast and over Nova Scotia and Newfoundland, in addition to a storm area over the North Atlantic.

On the morning of May 19th, a light rain was falling and the sky was overcast. Weather reports from land stations and ships along the great circle course were unfavorable and there was apparently no prospect of taking off for Paris for several days at least. In the morning I visited the Wright plant at Paterson, New Jersey, and had planned to attend a theatre performance in New York that evening. But at about six o'clock I received a special report from the New York Weather Bureau. A high pressure area was over the entire North Atlantic and the low pressure over Nova Scotia and

Newfoundland was receding. It was apparent that the pros-pects of the fog clearing up were as good as I might expect for some time to come. The North Atlantic should be clear with only local storms on the coast of Europe. The moon had just passed full and the percentage of days with fog over Newfoundland and the Grand Banks was increasing so that there seemed to be no advantage in waiting longer.

We went to Curtiss Field as quickly as possible and made arrangements for the barograph to be sealed and installed, and for the plane to be serviced and checked.

We decided partially to fill the fuel tanks in the hangar before towing the ship on a truck to Roosevelt Field, which adjoins Curtiss on the east, where the servicing would be completed.

I left the responsibility for conditioning the plane in the hands of the men on the field while I went into the hotel for about two and one-half hours of rest; but at the hotel there were several more details which had to be completed and I was unable to get any sleep that night.

I returned to the field before daybreak on the morning of the twentieth. A light rain was falling which continued until almost dawn; consequently we did not move the ship to Roosevelt Field until much later than we had planned, and the take-off was delayed from daybreak until nearly eight o'clock.

At dawn the shower had passed, although the sky was overcast, and occasionally there would be some slight pre-cipitation. The tail of the plane was lashed to a truck and escorted by a number of motorcycle police. The slow trip from Curtiss to Roosevelt was begun.

The ship was placed at the extreme west end of the field heading along the east and west runway, and the final fuel-ing commenced.

About 7:40 A.M. the motor was started and at 7:52 I took off on the flight for Paris.

The field was a little soft due to the rain during the night and the heavily loaded plane gathered speed very slowly. After passing the half-way mark, however, it was apparent that I would be able to clear the obstructions at the end. I passed over a tractor by about fifteen feet and a telephone line by about twenty, with a fair reserve of flying speed. I believe that the ship would have taken off from a hard field with at least five hundred pounds more weight.

I turned slightly to the right to avoid some high trees on a hill directly ahead, but by the time I had gone a few hundred yards I had sufficient altitude to clear all obstructions and throttled the engine down to 1750 R.P.M. I took up a compass course at once and soon reached Long Island Sound where the Curtiss Oriole with its photographer, which had been escorting me, turned back.

The haze soon cleared and from Cape Cod through the southern half of Nova Scotia the weather and visibility were excellent. I was flying very low, sometimes as close as ten feet from the trees and water.

On the three hundred mile stretch of water between Cape Cod and Nova Scotia I passed within view of numerous fishing vessels.

The northern part of Nova Scotia contained a number of storm areas and several times I flew through cloudbursts.

As I neared the northern coast, snow appeared in patches on the ground and far to the eastward the coastline was covered with fog.

For many miles between Nova Scotia and Newfoundland the ocean was covered with caked ice but as I approached the coast the ice disappeared entirely and I saw several ships in this area.

I had taken up a course for St. Johns, which is south of the great Circle from New York to Paris, so that there would be no question of the fact that I had passed Newfoundland in case I was forced down in the north Atlantic.

I passed over numerous icebergs after leaving St. Johns, but saw no ships except near the coast.

Darkness set in about 8:15 New York time and a thin, low fog formed through which the white bergs showed up with surprising clearness. This fog became thicker and increased in height until within two hours I was just skimming the top of storm clouds at about ten thousand feet. Even at this altitude there was a thick haze through which only the stars directly overhead could be seen.

There was no moon and it was very dark. The tops of some of the storm clouds were several thousand feet above me and at one time, when I attempted to fly through one of the larger clouds, sleet started to collect on the plane and I was forced to turn around and get back into clear air immediately and then fly around any clouds which I could not get over.

The moon appeared on the horizon after about two hours of darkness; then the flying was much less complicated.

Dawn came at about 1 A.M. New York time and the temperature had risen until there was practically no remaining danger of sleet.

Shortly after sunrise the clouds became more broken although some of them were far above me and it was often necessary to fly through them, navigating by instruments only.

As the sun became higher, holes appeared in the fog. Through one the open water was visible, and I dropped down until less than a hundred feet above the waves. There was a strong wind blowing from the northwest and the ocean was covered with white caps.

After a few miles of fairly clear weather the ceiling lowered to zero and for nearly two hours I flew entirely blind through the fog at an altitude of about 1500 feet. Then the fog raised and the water was visible again.

On several more occasions it was necessary to fly by instrument for short periods; then the fog broke up into patches.

These patches took on forms of every description. Numerous shorelines appeared, with trees perfectly outlined against the horizon. In fact, the mirages were so natural that, had I not been in mid-Atlantic and known that no land existed along my route, I would have taken them to be actual islands.

As the fog cleared I dropped down closer to the water, sometimes flying within ten feet of the waves and seldom higher than two hundred.

There is a cushion of air close to the ground or water through which a plane flies with less effort than when at a higher altitude, and for hours at a time I took advantage of this factor.

Also, it was less difficult to determine the wind drift near the water. During the entire flight the wind was strong enough to produce white caps on the waves. When one of these formed, the foam would be blown off, showing the wind's direction and approximate velocity. This foam remained on the water long enough for me to obtain a general idea of my drift.

During the day I saw a number of porpoises and a few birds but no ships, although I understand that two different boats reported me passing over.

The first indication of my approach to the European Coast was a small fishing boat which I first noticed a few miles ahead and slightly to the south of my course. There were several of these fishing boats grouped within a few miles of each other.

I flew over the first boat without seeing any signs of life. As I circled over the second, however, a man's face appeared, looking out of the cabin window.

I have carried on short conversations with people on the ground by flying low with throttled engine, shouting a question, and receiving the answer by some signal. When I saw this fisherman I decided to try to get him to point towards land. I had no sooner made the decision than the futility of the effort became apparent. In all likelihood he could not speak English, and even if he could he would undoubtedly be far too astounded to answer. However, I circled again and closing the throttle as the plane passed within a few feet of the boat I shouted, "Which way is Ireland?" Of course the attempt was useless, and I continued on my course.

Less than an hour later a rugged and semi-mountainous coastline appeared to the northeast. I was flying less than two hundred feet from the water when I sighted it. The shore was fairly distinct and not over ten or fifteen miles away. A light haze coupled with numerous local storm areas had prevented my seeing it from a long distance.

The coastline came down from the north, curved over towards the east. I had very little doubt that it was the south-western end of Ireland but in order to make sure I changed my course towards the nearest point of land.

I located Cape Valentia and Dingle Bay, then resumed my compass course towards Paris.

After leaving Ireland I passed a number of steamers and was seldom out of sight of a ship.

In a little over two hours the coast of England appeared. My course passed over Southern England and a little south of Plymouth; then across the English Channel, striking France over Cherbourg.

The English farms were very impressive from the air in contrast to ours in America. They appeared extremely small and unusually neat and tidy with their stone and hedge fences.

I was flying at about a fifteen hundred foot altitude over England and as I crossed the Channel and passed over Cherbourg, France, I had probably seen more of that part of Europe than many native Europeans. The visibility was good and the country could be seen for miles around.

People who have taken their first flight often remark that no one knows what the locality he lives in is like until he

has seen it from above. Countries take on different charac-
teristics from the air.

The sun went down shortly after passing Cherbourg and
soon the beacons along the Paris-London airway became
visible.

I first saw the lights of Paris a little before ten P.M., or
five P.M. New York time, and a few minutes later I was circling the Eiffel Tower at an altitude of about four thousand
feet.

The lights of Le Bourget were plainly visible, but appeared to be very close to Paris. I had understood that the
field was farther from the city, so continued out to the north-
east into the country for four or five miles to make sure that
there was not another field farther out which might be Le
Bourget. Then I returned and spiralled down closer to the
lights. Presently I could make out long lines of hangers, and
the roads appeared to be jammed with cars.

I flew low over the field once, then circled around into the
wind and landed.

After the plane stopped rolling I turned it around and
started to taxi back to the lights. The entire field ahead,
however, was covered with thousands of people all running
towards my ship. When the first few arrived, I attempted to
get them to hold the rest of the crowd back, away from the
plane, but apparently no one could understand, or would
have been able to conform to my request if he had.

I cut the switch to keep the propeller from killing some
one, and attempted to organize an impromptu guard for
the plane. The impossibility of any immediate organization
became apparent, and when parts of the ship began to crack
from the pressure of the multitude I decided to climb out of
the cockpit in order to draw the crowd away.

Speaking was impossible; no words could be heard in the
uproar and nobody apparently cared to hear any. I started
to climb out of the cockpit, but as soon as one foot appeared

through the door I was dragged the rest of the way without assistance on my part.

For nearly half an hour I was unable to touch the ground, during which time I was ardently carried around in what seemed to be a very small area, and in every position it is possible to be in. Every one had the best of intentions but no one seemed to know just what they were.

The French military flyers very resourcefully took the situation in hand. A number of them mingled with the crowd; then, at a given signal, they placed my helmet on an American correspondent and cried: "Here is Lindbergh." That helmet on an American was sufficient evidence. The correspondent immediately became the center of attraction, and while he was being taken protestingly to the Reception Committee via a rather devious route, I managed to get inside one of the hangars.

Meanwhile a second group of soldiers and police had surrounded the plane and soon placed it out of danger in another hangar.

The French ability to handle an unusual situation with speed and capability was remarkably demonstrated that night at Le Bourget.

AT THE MERCY OF THE BREAKERS

(From KON-TIKI: ACROSS THE PACIFIC BY RAFT. Chicago: Rand
McNally & Co., 1950)

*A new chapter in the modern history of navigation in the Pacific Ocean
was written when the raft Kon-Tiki, manned by five young men from
Norway and one from Sweden, sailed from Callao, Peru, to Raroia in
the Tuamotu Archipelago in Polynesia. In 101 days, the Kon-Tiki
covered 4,300 nautical miles, which is about the same distance as that
from Chicago to Moscow. The raft was composed basically of nine
great balsa logs lashed together with rope. Lighter logs of the same
buoyant wood were made fast crossways and the raft was decked with
split bamboo and mats of plaited bamboo reeds. The small cabin was
also of bamboo. The Kon-Tiki was forty-five feet long in the middle
and thirty feet at the sides. She carried a square sail and was steered
by means of a long stern oar and centerboards.*

*Thor Heyerdahl, the originator and leader of the expedition, de-
signed the Kon-Tiki to duplicate the structure of the rafts used by the
early South American Indians, and he recreated the conditions under
which these primitive seamen are thought to have migrated to the
islands of the South Pacific. In the account that follows, Heyerdahl
tells graphically how the remarkable voyage of the Kon-Tiki ended
when she was cast ashore in the breakers that lash the coral reef of
Raroia.*

We were drifting straight toward the ominous Takume and
Raroia reefs, which together blocked up forty to fifty miles
of the sea ahead of us. We made desperate efforts to steer
clear, to the north of these dangerous reefs, and things
seemed to be going well till one night the watch came hurrying in and called us all out.

The wind had changed. We were heading straight for the

Takume reef. It had begun to rain, and there was no visibility at all. The reef could not be far off.

In the middle of night we held a council of war. It was a question of saving our lives now. To get past on the north side was now hopeless; we must try to get through on the south side instead. We trimmed the sail, laid the oar over, and began a dangerous piece of sailing with the uncertain north wind behind us. If the east wind came back before we had passed the whole façade of the fifty-mile-long reefs, we should be hurled in among the breakers, at their mercy.

We agreed on all that should be done if shipwreck was imminent. We would stay on board the *Kon-Tiki* at all costs. We would not climb up the mast, from which we should be shaken down like rotten fruit, but would cling tight to the stays of the mast when the seas poured over us. We laid the rubber raft loose on the deck and made fast to it a small watertight radio transmitter, a small quantity of provisions, water bottles, and medical stores. This would be washed ashore independently of us if we ourselves should get over the reef safe but empty-handed. In the stern of the *Kon-Tiki* we made fast a long rope with a float which also would be washed ashore, so that we could try to pull in the raft if she were stranded out on the reef. And so we crept into bed and left the watch to the helmsman out in the rain.

As long as the north wind held, we glided slowly but surely down along the façade of the coral reefs which lay in ambush below the horizon. But then one afternoon the wind died away, and when it returned it had gone around into the east. According to Erik's position we were already so far down that we now had some hope of steering clear of the southernmost point of the Raroia reef. We would try to get round it and into shelter before going on to other reefs beyond it.

When night came, we had been a hundred days at sea.

Late in the night I woke, feeling restless and uneasy. There was something unusual in the movement of the waves. The

Kon-Tiki's motion was a little different from what it usually was in such conditions. We had become sensitive to changes in the rhythm of the logs. I thought at once of suction from a coast, which was drawing near, and was continually out on deck and up the mast. Nothing but sea was visible. But I could get no quiet sleep. Time passed.

At dawn, just before six, Torstein came hurrying down from the masthead. He could see a whole line of small palm-clad islands far ahead. Before doing anything else we laid the oar over to southward as far as we could. What Torstein had seen must be the small coral islands which lay strewn like pearls on a string behind the Raroia reef. A northward current must have caught us.

At half-past seven palm-clad islets had appeared in a row all along the horizon to westward. The southernmost lay roughly ahead of our bow, and thence there were islands and clumps of palms all along the horizon on our starboard side till they disappeared as dots away to northward. The nearest were four or five sea miles away.

A survey from the masthead showed that, even if our bow pointed toward the bottom island in the chain, our drift sideways was so great that we were not advancing in the direction in which our bow pointed. We were drifting diagonally right in toward the reef. With fixed centerboards we should still have had some hope of steering clear. But sharks were following close astern, so that it was impossible to dive under the raft and tighten up the loose centerboards with fresh guy ropes.

We saw that we had now only a few hours more on board the *Kon-Tiki*. They must be used in preparation for our inevitable wreck on the coral reef. Every man learned what he had to do when the moment came; each one of us knew where his own limited sphere of responsibility lay, so that we should not fly round treading on one another's toes when the time came and seconds counted. The *Kon-Tiki* pitched up and down, up and down, as the wind forced us in. There was no doubt that here was the turmoil of the waves created by the reef—some waves advancing while others were hurled back after beating vainly against the surrounding wall.

We were still under full sail in the hope of even now being able to steer clear. As we gradually drifted nearer, half sideways, we saw from the mast how the whole string of palm-clad isles was connected with a coral reef, part above and part under water, which lay like a mole where the sea was white with foam and leaped high into the air. The Raroia atoll is oval in shape and has a diameter of twenty-five miles, not counting the adjoining reefs of Takume. The whole of its longer side faces the sea to eastward, where we came pitching in. The reef itself, which runs in one line from horizon to horizon, is only a few hundred yards clear, and behind it idyllic islets lie in a string round the still lagoon inside.

It was with mixed feelings that we saw the blue Pacific being ruthlessly torn up and hurled into the air all along the horizon ahead of us. I knew what awaited us; I had visited the Tuamotu group before and had stood safe on land looking out over the immense spectacle in the east, where the surf from the open Pacific broke in over the reef. New reefs and islands kept on gradually appearing to southward. We must be lying off the middle of the façade of the coral wall.

On board the *Kon-Tiki* all preparations for the end of the voyage were being made. Everything of value was carried into the cabin and lashed fast. Documents and papers were packed into watertight bags, along with films and other things which would not stand a dip in the sea. The whole bamboo cabin was covered with canvas, and especially strong ropes were lashed across it. When we saw that all hope was gone, we opened up the bamboo deck and cut off with machete knives all the ropes which held the centerboards down. It was a hard job to get the centerboards drawn up, because they were all thickly covered with stout barnacles.

With the centerboards up the draught of our vessel was no deeper than to the bottom of the timber logs, and we would therefore be more easily washed in over the reef. With no centerboards and with the sail down, the raft lay completely sideways on and was entirely at the mercy of wind and sea.

We tied the longest rope we had to the homemade anchor and made it fast to the step of the port mast, so that the *Kon-Tiki* would go into the surf stern first when the anchor was thrown overboard. The anchor itself consisted of empty water cans filled with used radio batteries and heavy scrap, and solid mangrove-wood sticks projected from it, set crosswise.

Order number one, which came first and last, was: Hold on to the raft! Whatever happened, we must hang on tight on board and let the nine great logs take the pressure from the reef. We ourselves had more than enough to do to withstand the weight of the water. If we jumped overboard, we should become helpless victims of the suction which would fling us in and out over the sharp corals. The rubber raft would capsize in the steep seas or, heavily loaded with us in it, it would be torn to ribbons against the reef. But the wooden logs would sooner or later be cast ashore, and we with them, if we only managed to hold fast.

Next, all hands were told to put on their shoes for the first time in a hundred days and to have their life belts ready. The last precaution, however, was not of much value, for if a man fell overboard he would be battered to death, not drowned. We had time, too, to put our passports and such few dollars as we had left into our pockets. But it was not lack of time that was troubling us.

Those were anxious hours in which we lay drifting helplessly sideways, step after step, in toward the reef. It was noticeably quiet on board; we all crept in and out from cabin to bamboo deck, silent or laconic, and carried on with our jobs. Our serious faces showed that no one was in doubt as to what awaited us, and the absence of nervousness showed that we had all gradually acquired an unshakable confidence in the raft. If it had brought us across the sea, it would also manage to bring us ashore alive.

Inside the cabin there was a complete chaos of provision cartons and cargo, lashed fast. Torstein had barely found room for himself in the radio corner, where he had got the shortwave transmitter working. We were now over 4,000 sea miles from our old base at Callao, where the Peruvian Naval War School had maintained regular contact with us, and still farther from Hal and Frank and the other radio amateurs in the United States. But, as chance willed, we had on the previous day got in touch with a capable radio "ham" who had a set on Rarotonga in the Cook Islands, and the operators, quite contrary to all our usual practice, had arranged for an extra contact with him early in the morning. All the time we were drifting closer and closer in to the reef, Torstein was sitting tapping his key and calling Rarotonga.

Entries in the *Kon-Tiki's* log ran:

—*8:15: We are slowly approaching land. We can now make out with the naked eye the separate palm trees inside on the starboard side.*

—*8:45: The wind has veered into a still more unfavorable quarter for us, so we have no hope of getting clear. No nervousness on board, but hectic preparations on deck. There is something lying on the reef ahead of us which looks like the wreck of a sailing vessel, but it may be only a heap of driftwood.*

—*9:45: The wind is taking us straight toward the last island but one we see behind the reef. We now see the whole coral reef clearly; here it is built up like a white and red speckled wall which barely sticks up out of the water as a belt in front of all the islands. All along the reef white foaming surf is flung up toward the sky. Bengt is just serving up a good hot meal, the last before the great action!*

It is a wreck lying in there on the reef. We are so close now that

*we can see right across the shining lagoon behind the reef and see
the outlines of other islands on the other side of the lagoon.*

As this was written, the dull drone of the surf came near again;
it came from the whole reef and filled the air like thrilling rolls of
the drum, heralding the exciting last act of the *Kon-Tiki.*

*—9:50: Very close now. Drifting along the reef. Only a hundred
yards or so away. Torstein is talking to the man on Rarotonga. All
clear. Must pack up log now. All in good spirits; it looks bad,* but
we shall make it!

A few minutes later the anchor rushed overboard and
caught hold of the bottom, so that the *Kon-Tiki* swung
around and turned her stern inward toward the breakers. It
held us for a few valuable minutes, while Torstein sat ham-
mering like mad on the key. He had got Rarotonga now. The
breakers thundered in the air and the sea rose and fell
furiously. All hands were at work on deck, and now Torstein
got his message through. He said we were drifting toward
the Raroia reef. He asked Rarotonga to listen in on the same
wave length every hour. If we were silent for more than
thirty-six hours, Rarotonga must let the Norwegian Embassy
in Washington know. Torstein's last words were:

"O.K. Fifty yards left. Here we go. Good-by."

Then he closed down the station, Knut sealed up the
papers, and both crawled out on deck as fast as they could to
join the rest of us, for it was clear now that the anchor was
giving way.

The swell grew heavier and heavier, with deep troughs
between the waves, and we felt the raft being swung up and
down, up and down, higher and higher.

Again the order was shouted: "Hold on, never mind about
the cargo, hold on!"

We were now so near the waterfall inside that we no longer
heard the steady continuous roar from all along the reef. We
now heard only a separate boom each time the nearest
breaker crashed down on the rocks.

All hands stood in readiness, each clinging fast to the rope he thought the most secure. Only Erik crept into the cabin at the last moment; there was one part of the program he had not yet carried out—he had not found his shoes!

No one stood aft, for it was there the shock from the reef would come. Nor were the two firm stays which ran from the masthead down to the stern safe. For if the mast fell they would be left hanging overboard, over the reef. Herman, Bengt, and Torstein had climbed up on some boxes which were lashed forward of the cabin wall, and, while Herman clung on to the guy ropes from the ridge of the roof, the other two held on to the ropes from the masthead by which the sail at other times was hauled up. Knut and I chose the stay running from the bow up to the masthead, for, if mast and cabin and everything else went overboard, we thought the rope from the bow would nevertheless remain lying inboard, as we were now head on to the seas.

When we realized that the seas had got hold of us, the anchor rope was cut and we were off. A sea rose straight up under us, and we felt the *Kon-Tiki* being lifted up in the air. The great moment had come; we were riding on the wave back at breathless speed, our ramshackle craft creaking and groaning as she quivered under us. The excitement made one's blood boil. I remember that, having no other inspiration, I waved my arm and bellowed "Hurrah!" at the top of my lungs; it afforded a certain relief and could do no harm anyway. The others certainly thought I had gone mad, but they all beamed and grinned enthusiastically. On we ran with the seas rushing in behind us; this was the *Kon-Tiki's* baptism of fire. All must and would go well.

But our elation was soon dampened. A new sea rose high up astern of us like a glittering, green glass wall. As we sank down it came rolling after us, and, in the same second in which I saw it high above me, I felt a violent blow and was submerged under floods of water. I felt the suction through my whole body, with such great power that I had to strain

every single muscle in my frame and think of one thing only
—hold on, hold on! I think that in such a desperate situation
the arms will be torn off before the brain consents to let go,
evident as the outcome is. Then I felt that the mountain of
water was passing on and relaxing its devilish grip of my
body. When the whole mountain had rushed on, with an ear-
splitting roaring and crashing, I saw Knut again hanging on
beside me, doubled up into a ball. Seen from behind, the
great sea was almost flat and gray. As it rushed on, it swept
over the ridge of the cabin roof which projected from the
water, and there hung the three others, pressed against the
cabin roof as the water passed over them.

We were still afloat.

In an instant I renewed my hold, with arms and legs bent
round the strong rope. Knut let himself down and with a
tiger's leap joined the others on the boxes, where the cabin
took the strain. I heard reassuring exclamations from them,
but at the same time I saw a new green wall rise up and come
towering toward us. I shouted a warning and made myself
as small and hard as I could where I hung. In an instant hell
was over us again, and the *Kon-Tiki* disappeared completely
under the masses of water. The sea tugged and pulled with
all the force it could bring to bear at the poor little bundles
of human bodies. The second sea rushed over us, to be followed by a third like it.

Then I heard a triumphant shout from Knut, who was now
hanging on to the rope ladder:

"Look at the raft—she's holding!"

After three seas only the double mast and the cabin had
been knocked a bit crooked. Again we had a feeling of triumph over the elements, and the elation of victory gave us
new strength.

Then I saw the next sea come towering up, higher than all
the rest, and again I bellowed a warning aft to the others as
I climbed up the stay, as high as I could get in a hurry, and
hung on fast. Then I myself disappeared sideways into the

midst of the green wall which towered high over us. The others, who were farther aft and saw me disappear first, estimated the height of the wall of water at twenty-five feet, while the foaming crest passed by fifteen feet above the part of the glassy wall into which I had vanished. Then the great wave reached them, and we had all one single thought —hold on, hold on, hold, hold, hold!

We must have hit the reef that time. I myself felt only the strain on the stay, which seemed to bend and slacken jerkily. But whether the bumps came from above or below I could not tell, hanging there. The whole submersion lasted only seconds, but it demanded more endurance than we usually have in our bodies. There is greater strength in the human mechanism than that of the muscles alone. I determined that, if I was to die, I would die in this position, like a knot on the stay. The sea thundered on, over and past, and as it roared by it revealed a hideous sight. The *Kon-Tiki* was wholly changed, as by the stroke of a magic wand. The vessel we knew from weeks and months at sea was no more; in a few seconds our pleasant world had become a shattered wreck.

I saw only one man on board besides myself. He lay pressed flat across the ridge of the cabin roof, face downward with his arms stretched out on both sides, while the cabin itself was crushed in, like a house of cards, toward the stern and toward the starboard side. The motionless figure was Herman. There was no other sign of life, while the hill of water thundered by, in across the reef. The hardwood mast on the starboard side was broken like a match, and the upper stump, in its fall, had smashed right through the cabin roof, so that the mast and all its gear slanted at a low angle over the reef on the starboard side. Astern, the steering block was twisted round lengthways and the crossbeam broken, while the steering oar was smashed to splinters. The splashboards at the bow were broken like cigar boxes, and the whole deck was torn up and pasted like wet paper against the forward wall of the cabin, along with boxes, cans, canvas, and other

cargo. Bamboo sticks and rope ends stuck up everywhere, and the general effect was of complete chaos.

I felt cold fear run through my whole body. What was the good of my holding on? If I lost one single man here, in the run in, the whole thing would be ruined, and for the moment there was only one human figure to be seen after the last buffet. In that second Torstein's hunched-up form appeared outside the raft. He was hanging like a monkey in the ropes from the masthead and managed to get on to the logs again, where he crawled up on to the debris forward of the cabin. Herman, too, now turned his head and gave me a forced grin of encouragement, but did not move. I bellowed in the faint hope of locating the others and heard Bengt's calm voice call out that all hands were aboard. They were lying holding on to the ropes behind the tangled barricade which the tough plaiting from the bamboo deck had built up.

All this happened in the course of a few seconds, while the *Kon-Tiki* was being drawn out of the witches' caldron by the backwash, and a fresh sea came rolling over her. For the last time I bellowed "Hang on!" at the top of my lungs amid the uproar, and that was all I myself did; I hung on and disappeared in the masses of water which rushed over and past in those endless two or three seconds. That was enough for me. I saw the ends of the logs knocking and bumping against a sharp step in the coral reef without going over it. Then we were sucked out again. I also saw the two men who lay stretched out across the ridge of the cabin roof, but none of us smiled any longer. Behind the chaos of bamboo I heard a calm voice call out:

"This won't do."

I myself felt equally discouraged. As the masthead sank farther and farther out over the starboard side, I found myself hanging on to a slack line outside the raft. The next sea came. When it had gone by I was dead tired, and my only thought was to get up on to the logs and lie behind the barricade. When the backwash retreated, I saw for the first time the rugged red reef naked beneath us and perceived Torstein standing, bent double, on gleaming red corals, holding on to a bunch of rope ends from the mast. Knut, standing aft, was about to jump. I shouted that we must all keep on the logs, and Torstein, who had been washed overboard by the pressure of water, sprang up again like a cat.

Two or three more seas rolled over us with diminishing force, and what happened then I do not remember, except that water foamed in and out and I myself sank lower and lower toward the red reef over which we were being lifted in. Then only crests of foam full of salt spray came whirling in, and I was able to work my way in on to the raft, where we all made for the after end of the logs which was highest up on the reef.

At the same moment Knut crouched down and sprang up on to the reef with the line which lay clear astern. While the backwash was running out, he waded through the whirling water some thirty yards in and stood safely at the end of the line when the next sea foamed in toward him, died down, and ran back from the flat reef like a broad stream.

Then Erik came crawling out of the collapsed cabin, with his shoes on. If we had all done as he did, we should have got off cheaply. As the cabin had not been washed overboard but had been pressed down pretty flat under the canvas, Erik lay quietly stretched out among the cargo and heard the peals of thunder crashing above him while the collapsed bamboo walls curved downward. Bengt had had a slight concussion when the mast fell but had managed to crawl under the wrecked cabin alongside Erik. We should all of us have been lying there if we had realized in advance how firmly the countless lashings and plaited bamboo sheets would hang on to the main logs under the pressure of the water.

Erik was now standing ready on the logs aft, and when the sea retired he, too, jumped up on to the reef. It was Herman's turn next, and then Bengt's. Each time the raft was pushed a bit farther in, and, when Torstein's turn and my own came, the raft already lay so far in on the reef that there was no longer any ground for abandoning her. All hands began the work of salvage.

We were now twenty yards away from that devilish step up on the reef, and it was there and beyond it that the breakers came rolling after one another in long lines. The coral polyps had taken care to build the atoll so high that only the very tops of the breakers were able to send a fresh stream of sea water past us and into the lagoon, which abounded in fish. Here inside was the coral's own world, and they disported themselves in the strangest shapes and colors.

A long way in on the reef the others found the rubber raft, lying drifting and quite waterlogged. They emptied it and dragged it back to the wreck, and we loaded it to the full with the most important equipment, like the radio set, provisions, and water bottles. We dragged all this in across the reef and piled it up on the top of a huge block of coral, which lay alone on the inside of the reef like a large meteorite. Then we went back to the wreck for fresh loads. We could never know what the sea would be up to when the tidal currents got to work around us.

In the shallow water inside the reef we saw something bright shining in the sun. When we waded over to pick it up, to our astonishment we saw two empty tins. This was not exactly what we had expected to find there, and we were still more surprised when we saw that the little boxes were quite bright and newly opened and stamped "Pineapple," with the same inscription as that on the new field rations we ourselves were testing for the quartermaster. They were indeed two of our own pineapple tins which we had thrown overboard after our last meal on board the *Kon-Tiki*. We had followed close behind them up on the reef.

We were standing on sharp, rugged coral blocks, and on the uneven bottom we waded now ankle-deep, now chest-deep, according to the channels and stream beds in the reef.

Anemones and corals gave the whole reef the appearance of a rock garden covered with mosses and cactus and fossilized plants, red and green and yellow and white. There was no color that was not represented, either in corals or algae or in shells and sea slugs and fantastic fish, which were wriggling about everywhere. In the deeper channels small sharks about four feet long came sneaking up to us in the crystal-clear water. But we had only to smack the water with the palms of our hands for them to turn about and keep at a distance.

Where we had stranded, we had only pools of water and wet patches of coral about us; farther in lay the calm blue lagoon. The tide was going out, and we continually saw more corals sticking up out of the water round us, while the surf which thundered without interruption along the reef sank down, as it were, a floor lower. What would happen there on the narrow reef when the tide began to flow again was uncertain. We must get away.

The reef stretched like a half-submerged fortress wall up to the north and down to the south. In the extreme south was a long island densely covered with tall palm forest. And just above us to the north, only 600 or 700 yards away, lay another but considerably smaller palm island. It lay inside the reef, with palm tops rising into the sky and snow-white sandy beaches running out into the still lagoon. The whole island looked like a bulging green basket of flowers, or a little bit of concentrated paradise.

This island we chose.

Herman stood beside me beaming all over his bearded face. He did not say a word, only stretched out his hand and laughed quietly. The *Kon-Tiki* still lay far out on the reef with the spray flying over her. She was a wreck, but an honorable wreck. Everything above deck was smashed up, but the nine balsa logs from the Quevedo forest in Ecuador were as intact as ever. They had saved our lives.

HEINRICH HARRER

THE DALAI LAMA, BOY RULER OF TIBET

(From SEVEN YEARS IN TIBET. New York: E. P. Dutton & Co., Inc., 1953)

Lhasa, capital of Tibet, is known as the Forbidden City and is the most mysterious capital in the world. Few Westerners have ever visited it, for foreigners are barred from the country and all roads to Lhasa are closely guarded. Yet Heinrich Harrer, a noted Austrian mountaineer, had the experience of living in Tibet for seven years! After escaping during World War II from an internment camp in India, Harrer and a companion, Peter Aufschnaiter, succeeded in reaching Lhasa after a long, adventurous journey of many months through the high mountains and across the lofty plateau country of Tibet. Once in the capital, they were granted asylum and were hospitably treated by the highest Tibetan circles. Eventually Harrer was employed in Lhasa to do landscape gardening in the grounds of the Norbulingka, summer residence of the God-King of Tibet, the Dalai Lama. He also built a private motion picture theater in the park. The Dalai Lama, whom his subjects regard as the Living Buddha, was then only fourteen years old. In the following passage from his book, Harrer tells of his friendship with the young ruler of Tibet.

When the spring came the Norbulingka was a vision of loveliness. The peach and pear blossoms were in full bloom. Peacocks strutted proudly through the grounds and hundreds of rare plants stood in pots in the sunshine. In one corner of the park there was a small zoo, but most of the cages were empty. Only a few wildcats and lynxes remained. Formerly there were panthers and bears, but these had soon succumbed in their narrow dens. The Dalai Lama received many presents of wild animals, especially injured ones, which found a safe refuge in the Jeweled Garden.

In addition to the temples there were many small houses scattered about under the trees. Each was used for a special purpose—one was for meditation, another for reading and study, and others served as meeting places for the monks. The largest building, several stories high, stood in the center of the garden and was half a temple and half a residence for His Holiness. The windows were too small for my liking, and I found the title "palace" too flattering for this ordinary house. It was certainly more attractive as a residence than the Potala, which was more like a prison than a palace, but it was rather dark. So was the garden. The trees had been allowed to grow untended for many years and in places they resembled a dense jungle. No one had ever attempted to clear them out. The gardeners complained that flowers and fruit simply would not grow in the shade of the big trees. I would have been very happy if they had allowed me to tidy up and rearrange the Inner Garden. There were many gardeners, but none with a sense of style. I did succeed in convincing the high chamberlain that certain trees had to be cut down and I was allowed to supervise the work of felling them. The gardeners had little understanding of this sort of thing, and occupied themselves mainly with cultivating pot flowers, which were left out in the open all day and placed under cover at night.

One of the doors in the wall of the Inner Garden led directly to the stables, which housed the favorite horses of the Dalai Lama and an onager which had been presented to him. These animals lived a contemplative, peaceful life tended by many grooms. They grew fat and soft as their master never rode or drove them.

The teachers and personal servants of the Dalai Lama lived outside the yellow wall in the Norbulingka park. They and the bodyguard, five hundred strong, lived in comfortable and (for Tibet) extraordinarily clean blocks of houses. The thirteenth Dalai Lama had taken a personal interest in the welfare of his troops. He had dressed them in uniforms of European cut and used to watch them exercising from one of his pavilions. I was struck by the fact that these soldiers had their hair cut in Western fashion in contrast to all other Tibetans. The thirteenth Dalai Lama had probably been favorably impressed by the appearance of British and Indian troops during his stay in India and had modeled his bodyguard on them. The officers lived in nice little bungalows with flower beds blooming all around them. The duties of officers and men were easy. They consisted mainly of mounting guard and turning out to march in ceremonial processions.

Long before the Dalai Lama moved into the Summer Residence I had finished my building. I wondered if he would be pleased with the theater. I could count on learning his opinion of it all from Lobsang Samten, who was certain to be present at the first performance. The Dalai Lama would probably call on the film man of the Indian Legation to work the apparatus. The legation used frequently to show films, Indian and English, at its pleasant parties and it was a joy to see the childish enthusiasm with which the Tibetans watched these performances and especially the films showing scenes from distant lands. The question was how the young ruler would react to the pictures.

I was naturally present with my moving-picture camera to see the procession from the Potala to the Norbulingka. I had the usual difficulty in finding a suitable place from which to film the ceremony, but my attendant, a pock-marked giant of formidable aspect, made things easier for me. He carried my cameras and the crowds opened to let us through. He not only looked forbidding, but was in fact a very gallant fellow as the following anecdote shows.

It sometimes happens that leopards stray into the gardens of Lhasa. They must not be killed, so the people try to lure them into traps or catch them by any sort of device. One day a leopard got through into the Garden of Jewels. Harried on all sides and wounded in the foot by a bullet, it was driven into a corner where it stood at bay spitting at anyone who dared to approach it. Suddenly my attendant went for it with his bare hands and held it until other soldiers rushed up with a sack into which they forced it. The man was badly clawed and the leopard was lodged in the Dalai Lama's zoo, where it soon died.

When the Dalai Lama passed by me in his sedan chair and found me filming he gave me a smile. My private thought was that he was congratulating himself on his little motion-picture theater, but I am sure that no one else thought as I did; though what could be more natural for a lonely fourteen-year-old boy? Then a look at the humble and rapturous face of my attendant reminded me that for everyone else except myself, he was not a lonely boy but a god.

After filming the scenes in the Norbulingka I was riding slowly home when, a little way out of Lhasa, I was over-hauled by an excited soldier of the bodyguard, who told me that they had been looking for me everywhere and that I must at once ride back to the Summer Garden. My first thought was that the motion-picture apparatus was out of order, as I could hardly imagine that the young ruler, still a minor, would override all conventions and summon me directly to see him. I immediately turned around and was soon back at the Norbulingka, where everything was now peaceful and still. At the door of the yellow gate a couple of monks were waiting. As soon as they saw me they signaled to me to hurry up and when I reached them they ushered me into the Inner Garden. There Lobsang Samten awaited me. He whispered something to me and put a white scarf in my hand. There was no doubt about it. His brother was going to receive me.

I at once went toward the motion-picture theater, but before I could enter the door opened from the inside and I was standing before the Living Buddha. Conquering my surprise I bowed deeply and handed him the scarf. He took it in his left hand and with an impulsive gesture blessed me with his right. It seemed less like the ceremonial laying on of hands than an impetuous expression of feeling on the part of a boy who had at last got his way. In the theater three abbots were waiting with bowed heads—the guardians of His Holiness. I knew them all well and did not fail to observe how coldly they returned my greeting. They certainly did not approve of this intrusion into their domain, but they had not dared openly to oppose the will of the Dalai Lama.

The young ruler was all the more cordial. He beamed all over his face and poured out a flood of questions. He seemed to me like a person who had for years brooded in solitude over different problems, and now that he had at last someone to talk to, wanted to know all the answers at once. He gave me no time to think over my answers, but pressed me to go to the projector and put on a film which he had long been wanting to see. It was a documentary film of the capitulation of Japan. He came with me to the apparatus and sent the abbots into the theater to act as spectators.

I must have seemed slow and clumsy in handling the projector as he impatiently pushed me on one side and, taking hold of the film, showed me that he was a much more practiced operator than I was. He told me that he had been busy the whole winter learning how to work the apparatus and that he had even taken a projector to pieces and put it together again. I observed then, for the first time, that he liked to get to the bottom of things instead of taking them for granted. And so, later on, like many a good father who wishes to earn the respect of his son, I often spent the evening reviving my knowledge of half-forgotten things or studying new ones. I took the utmost trouble to treat every question seriously and scientifically, as it was clear to me that my answers would form the basis of his knowledge of the Western world.

His obvious talent for technical things astonished me at our first meeting. It was a masterly performance for a boy of fourteen years to take a projector to pieces and then to reassemble it without any help, for he could not read the English prospectus. Now that the film was running well, he was delighted with the arrangements and could not praise my work too highly. We sat together in the projecting room and looked at the picture through the peep holes in the wall and he took the greatest pleasure in what he saw and heard, often clasping my hands excitedly with the vivacity of youth. Although it was the first time in his life that he had been alone with a white man he was in no way embarrassed or shy. While he was putting the next film on the reel, he pressed the microphone into my hands and insisted on my speaking into it. At the same time he looked through the peep holes into the electrically lit theater in which his tutors sat on carpets. I could see how keen he was to observe the wondering faces of the worthy abbots when a voice should suddenly come out of the loudspeaker. I did not want to disappoint him so I invited the nonexistent public to remain in their seats as the next film would present sensational scenes from Tibet. He laughed enthusiastically at the surprised and shocked faces of the monks when they heard my cheerful, disrespectful tones. Such light, unceremonious language had never been used in the presence of the Divine Ruler, whose gleaming eyes showed how much he enjoyed the situation.

He made me turn the film which I had made in Lhasa while he looked after the switches. I was as curious as he was to see the results, as this was my first full-length picture. An expert could have picked out faults in it, but it seemed quite satisfactory to us. It contained my shots of the "little" New Year Festival. Even the formal abbots forgot their dignity when they recognized themselves on the flickering screen.

There was a burst of laughter when a full-length picture appeared of a minister who had gone to sleep during the ceremonies. There was no malice in their laughter, for each of the abbots had sometimes to struggle to keep awake during these endless festivities. All the same the upper classes must have got to know that the Dalai Lama had witnessed his minister's weakness, for afterwards whenever I appeared with my camera, everyone sat up and posed.

The Dalai Lama himself took more pleasure than anyone in the pictures. His usually slow movements became youthful and lively and he commented enthusiastically on every picture. After a while I asked him to turn a film which he had made himself. He very modestly said that he would not dare to show his apprentice efforts after the pictures we had already seen. But I was anxious to see what subjects he had chosen for filming and persuaded him to put his roll onto the screen. He had not, of course, had a large choice of subjects. He had done a big sweeping landscape of the valley of Lhasa, which he turned much too fast. Then came a few under-lighted long-distance pictures of mounted noblemen and caravans passing through Shö. A close-up of his cook showed that he would have liked to take film portraits. The film he had shown me was absolutely his first attempt and had been made without instructions or help. When it was over he got me to announce through the microphone that the performance was over. He then opened the door leading into the theater, told the abbots that he did not need them any more and dismissed them with a wave of the hand. It was again clear to me that here was no animated puppet, but a clear-cut individual will capable of imposing itself on others.

When we were alone we cleared away the films and put the yellow covers on the machines. Then we sat down on a magnificent carpet in the theater with the sun streaming through the open windows. It was fortunate that I had long acquired the habit of sitting cross-legged, as chairs and cushions are not included in the Dalai Lama's household furniture. At the start I had wished to decline his invitation to sit down, knowing that even ministers were not supposed to sit in his presence, but he just took me by the sleeve and pulled me down, which put an end to my misgivings.

He told me that he had long been planning this meeting as he had not been able to think of any other way of becoming acquainted with the outside world. He expected the regent to raise objections but he was determined to have his own way and had already thought up a rejoinder in case of opposition. He was resolved to extend his knowledge beyond purely religious subjects, and it seemed to him that I was the person who could help him to do so. He had no idea that I was a qualified teacher, and had he known this it would probably not have influenced him. He asked my age and was surprised to learn that I was only thirty-seven. Like many Tibetans he thought that my "yellow" hair was a sign of age. He studied my features with childish curiosity and teased me about my long nose, which, though of normal size as we reckon noses, had often attracted the attention of the snub-nosed Mongolians. At last he noticed that I had hair growing on the back of my hands and said with a broad grin: "Henrig, you have hair like a monkey." I had an answer ready, as I was familiar with the legend that the Tibetans derive their descent from the union of their god Chenrezi with a female demon. Before coupling with his demon lover Chenrezi had assumed the shape of a monkey, and since the Dalai Lama is one of the Incarnations of this god, I found that in comparing me with an ape he had really flattered me.

With remarks such as this our conversation soon became unconstrained and we both lost our shyness. I now felt the attraction of his personality, which at our earlier fleeting contacts I had only guessed at. His complexion was much lighter than that of the average Tibetan. His eyes, hardly narrower than those of most Europeans, were full of expression, charm, and vivacity. His cheeks glowed with excitement, and as he sat he kept sliding from side to side. His ears stood out a little from his head. This was a characteristic of the Buddha and, as I learned later, was one of the signs by which as a child he had been recognized as an incarnation. His hair was longer than is customary. He probably wore it so as a protection against the cold of the Potala. He was tall for his age and looked as though he would reach the stature of his parents, both of whom had striking figures. Unfortunately, as a result of much study in a seated posture with his body bent forward, he held himself badly. He had beautiful aristocratic hands with long fingers which were generally folded in an attitude of peace. I noticed that he often looked at my hands with astonishment when I emphasized what I was saying with a gesture. Gesticulation is entirely foreign to the Tibetans, who in their reposeful attitudes express the calm of Asia. He always wore the red robe of a monk, once prescibed by Buddha, and his costume differed in no way from that of the monastic officials.

Time passed swiftly. It seemed as if a dam had burst, so urgent and continuous was the flood of questions which he put to me. I was astounded to see how much disconnected knowledge he had acquired out of books and newspapers. He possessed an English work on the Second World War in seven volumes, which he had had translated into Tibetan. He knew how to distinguish between different types of airplanes, automobiles, and tanks. The names of personages like Churchill, Eisenhower, and Molotov were familiar to him, but as he had nobody to put questions to, he often did not know how persons and events were connected with each other. Now he was happy, because he had found someone to whom he could bring all the questions about which he had been puzzling for years.

It must have been about three o'clock when Sopön Khenpo came in to say that it was time to eat. This was the abbot whose duty it was to look after the physical welfare of the Dalai Lama. When he gave his message, I immediately rose to my feet meaning to take my leave, but the God-King drew me down again and told the abbot to come again later. He then, very modestly took out an exercise book with all sorts of drawings on the cover and asked me to look at his work. To my surprise I saw that he had been transcribing the capital letters of the Latin alphabet. What versatility and what initiative! Strenuous religious studies, tinkering with complicated mechanical appliances, and now modern languages! He insisted that I should immediately begin to teach him English, transcribing the pronunciation in elegant Tibetan characters. Another hour must have passed, when Sopön Khenpo came in again and this time insisted that his master should take his dinner. He had a dish of cakes, white bread, and sheep's cheese in his hand which he pressed on me. As I wanted to refuse it, he rolled the food up in a white cloth for me to take home with me.

But the Dalai Lama still did not want to end our conversation. In wheedling tones he begged his cupbearer to wait a little longer. With a loving look at his charge the abbot agreed and left us. I had the feeling that he was as fond of the boy and as devoted as if he had been his father. This white-haired ancient had served the thirteenth Dalai Lama in the same capacity and had remained in the service. This was a great tribute to his trustworthiness and loyalty, for in Tibet when there is a change of masters, there is a change of servants. The Dalai Lama proposed that I should visit his family who lived in the Norbulingka during the summer. He told me to wait in their house till he should send for me. When I left him he shook my hand warmly—a new gesture for him.

As I walked through the empty garden and pushed back the gate bolts, I could hardly realize that I had just spent five hours with the God-King of Lama Land. A gardener shut the gate behind me and the guard, which had been changed more than once since I came in, presented arms in some surprise. I rode slowly back to Lhasa and, but for the bundle of cakes which I was carrying, I would have thought it was all a dream. Which of my friends would have believed me if I had told him that I had just spent several hours alone in conversation with the Dalai Lama?

Needless to say I was very happy in the new duties that had fallen to my lot. To instruct this clever lad—the ruler of a land as big as France, Spain, and Germany put together—in the knowledge and science of the Western world, seemed a worthwhile task, to say the least.

On the same evening I looked up some reviews which contained details of the construction of jet planes, about which my young pupil had that day asked me questions to which I did not know the answers. I had promised to give him full explanations at our next meeting. As time went on I always prepared the materials for our lessons, as I wanted to introduce some system into the instruction of this zealous student.

I had many setbacks on account of his insatiable curiosity, which drove him to ask me questions that opened up whole new fields. Many of these questions I could answer only to the best of my knowledge. In order, for example, to be able to discuss the atom bomb, I had to tell him about the elements. That led to a formal discussion on metals, for which there is no generic word in Tibetan, so I had to go into details about the different sorts of metals—a subject which, of course, brought down an avalanche of questions.

My life in Lhasa had now begun a new phase. My existence had an aim. I no longer felt unsatisfied or incomplete. I did not abandon my former duties. I still collected news for the ministry: I still drew maps. But now the days were all too short and I often worked till late into the night. I had little time for pleasures and hobbies, for when the Dalai Lama called me, I had to be free. Instead of going to parties in the morning, as others did, I came late in the afternoon. But that was no sacrifice. I was happy in the consciousness that my life had a goal. The hours I spent with my pupil were as instructive for me as they were for him. He taught me a great deal about the history of Tibet and the teachings of Buddha. He was a real authority on these subjects. We often used to argue for hours on religious subjects and he was convinced that he would succeed in converting me to Buddhism. He told me that he was making a study of books containing knowledge of the ancient mysteries by which the body and the soul could be separated. The history of Tibet is full of stories about saints whose spirits used to perform actions hundreds of miles away from their physical bodies. The Dalai Lama was convinced that by virtue of his faith and by performing the prescribed rites he would be able to make things happen in far-distant places like Samye. When he had made sufficient progress, he said he would send me there and direct me from Lhasa. I remember saying to him with a laugh "All right, Kundün, when you can do that, I will become a Buddhist too."

NORBERT CASTERET

DE PROFUNDIS: 1954

(From THE DESCENT OF PIERRE SAINT-MARTIN. New York: Philo-
sophical Library, Inc., 1956)

*The year 1953 was remarkable because in that year men climbed
Everest, the highest mountain in the world, and also descended into
the deepest known chasm. Speleology is the name given to the scientific
exploration of caves. In 1952 a party of French speleologists set out to
explore an enormous chasm in the Basque country of France known as
Pierre Saint-Martin. During the descent Marcel Loubens lost his life.
The book from which the extract that follows is taken tells how his
friends came back to recover his body which had been left in the cave,
and at the same time carry on the exploration so tragically interrupted.*

I reached Pierre Saint-Martin on 3rd August 1954, a whole
day in advance of my companions. Two Spanish *carabiniers*
stood near the entry to the pot-hole. These men were wrapped
in heavy cloaks, for the weather was grey and cold as it so
often was throughout that dreary summer. They had been
on guard for several days, taking turns of duty with four
others under the command of a lieutenant.

At the bottom of the shake-hole (a depression about 30
feet deep giving access to the narrow opening of the shaft
itself) I could see the wooden cross upon which, in 1952, we
had painted these words: 'In the depths of this chasm lies
Marcel Loubens, fallen on the battlefield of speleology.'

Wind, rain, snow, and sun had obliterated much of the inscription, and I noticed that the first line 'In the depths of
this chasm lies . . .' had completely vanished. The coinci-

dence struck me, and I chose to regard it as a favorable omen of our purpose: Loubens would rest no more in that vast, cruel abyss; we would succeed in bringing up his body, and give it Christian burial at long last in the cemetery of his native village. We had given his parents a solemn promise to that effect in 1952.

4th August. The sun rose in a cloudless sky; and while the last of our party hurried up from the valley to the camp, pitched at an altitude of 5,800 feet, the drone of approaching aircraft could be heard. As in 1953, the Air Force and Parachute Regiment at Pau had kindly agreed to deliver our heavier and more cumbersome gear by parachute.

Three Junkers machines made several journeys to drop some fifty loads. They fulfilled their task with incomparable skill; for in spite of strong winds and the slope on which we were assembled, the multi-coloured parachutes came down literally into our arms. A single tourist plane carrying a press photographer, together with an observation-aircraft circled overhead throughout the morning. The whole business, in fact, looked like an aerial display staged for the benefit of all—shepherds, sight-seers, speleologists, French and Spanish police. The most important and most fragile load came down in twin parachutes joined together, and landed gently on the grass. This was the duralumin container; it measured 7 feet 6 inches in length, and was made at the École Pratique at Bagnères-de-Bigorre to Lépineux's design.

Later in the day a convoy of mules brought up the remainder of our gear, which we stored near the shepherd's hut. For the fifth successive year the hum of activity caused by our arrival had disturbed the solitude and silence of the Pyrenees.

Tents sprang up like mushrooms; packing cases that lay where they had fallen from the air were now collected by members of the team, and by a crowd of trippers who lent a willing hand but who were obliged to beat a hasty retreat on the approach of bad weather. Mist rose stealthily from the valley and enshrouded everything. Torrential rain driven by an icy wind brought the day to a miserable close; reminding us that we were indeed high up on the western Pyrenees, where the Atlantic gales provide an annual rainfall of something like ninety-six inches. Lévi had warned us in the circular letter before the expedition: 'Waterproof clothing will of course be no less essential in the surface camp than at the bottom of the chasm.'

5th and 6th August. These were days of preparation, during which everyone worked hard at all kinds of jobs: laying telephone lines; erecting the heavy winding-gear at the mouth of the shaft; repairing tackle which had been damaged in transit; packing materials and foodstuffs for use underground. Last, but not least, our cooks got busy laying out their kitchen.

There were twenty members of the team. Most of us had not met for twelve months; for the Groupe Spéléologique de la Pierre Saint-Martin, which includes men from all over France and Belgium, makes a point of foregathering only once a year, on the occasion of its summer campaign.

6th August. The Spanish lieutenant climbed up from his little camp 220 yards from the pot-hole. His manner was quite formal; he simply wanted a full list of the party. Then, to our absolute amazement he gave us official notice that the Spaniards would take no part in the expedition, and that we must confine ourselves to recovering Loubens's body—there must be no further attempt to explore the chasm.

By nightfall, Queffelec, with his assistants, Rossini, Isola, Accoce, and Laisse, had got the winch into position. Pierre Louis, our official engineer, set a pulley-jack at the entry to

the great vertical shaft. All was now ready, and the descent
could begin.

I had again volunteered to go down first, both as a matter
of principle and also to clear the cornices of fallen stone. This
particular chasm . . . is still in process of formation; from
year to year masses of rock break off from the walls and pile
up in dangerous heaps on the balconies and smaller overhangs. Lépineux, however, had determined to lighten my
task by cleaning the first platform, 263 feet down. He
reached it without mishap, and set to work with an American army shovel, conversing with us over the telephone
meanwhile. I was at the receiving end, not far from the
winch; I took note of all he said, and I must say it surprised
me. Considering he had himself cleared this same balcony,
which inclined sharply downward, he was amazed by the
amount of debris that had accumulated since 1953. He spent
a good two hours throwing down lumps of rock; and I could
hear his gasps of astonishment as he realized the extent to
which the interior of the chasm had disintegrated.

You see, nothing can fall into the shaft from outside; the
entrance is far too narrow, and opens like a dormer-window
in a vertical wall of rock. All this debris with which Lépineux
had to deal came from *inside*, through 'chimneys' and smaller
flues crammed with stones. These were gradually dislodged
by the trickling water and erosion, and fell into the shaft.

As darkness fell it grew cold, a keen wind blew, and a dismal fog lay heavy on the mountain. 'Real Pierre Saint-Martin
weather,' as someone had remarked as we returned to camp
for the night. A small, solitary tent drowned in mist, and
shaken by angry squalls, is not an enchanting or invigorat-
ing place.

Alone, rolled up in my sleeping-bag, I could still hear
within me those subterranean avalanches hurtling downward, smashed to fragments at terrifying depths. I saw myself tomorrow, within a few short hours, hanging from a

thread in that huge shaft which a Parisian journalist had so aptly described as 'the Eiffel Tower poised on the towers of Notre Dame.'

7th August. A bright, sunny day. I could hear sheepbells in the neighbouring fold; there were voices too, one of them Etchebarre's. That worthy *gendarme* was busy sending radio messages by short-wave to Saint-Engrâce in the valley.

Attention was before long concentrated upon the shake-hole, where Queffelec shouted to his assistants and then asked in a tremendous voice: 'Anyone for the lift?' 'Shan't be long!' I called back, knowing to whom his question was directed. Then, while the rest of the party moved towards the chasm, I disappeared into a stone hut where the provisions were stored. Henri Périllous, our cook, was busied about many things; he was the least talkative, but one of the hardest working members of our crew. Throughout our stay at Pierre Saint-Martin this frail, retiring youth of eighteen, ever willing and ever smiling, fulfilled a crushing task. He was always on duty, cooking at all hours of the day and night, or carrying pails of water from a distant stream. In fact, Henri Périllous had often to go down to the winch in the middle of the night with food for hungry workers who could not leave their job.

'Henri,' I said, 'I'm going down in half an hour'; and the good fellow at once lit another stove* and prepared me an excellent lunch. (It was unlikely that I should have another hot meal for a week!) I had even to refuse a second course; there was too much of it, and I was going to need all my resources of mind and body for my journey down the shaft.

It was 10 a.m. by the time I reached the shake-hole.

Before going down the shake-hole on a rope-ladder, I stopped for a word with Queffelec and to cast an eye over the winding-gear. Its strength reassured me; but not being

---

* These stoves were fuelled with butane gas.

an engineer I understood little of its complicated mechanism. Queffelec drew me aside, and, lowering his normally loud voice, pointed to the new steel cable on its drum: 'It's not as good as last year's,' he said. 'It's quite safe, of course, but the strands are not so tightly wound. I warn you, you'll spin round like a top.' This was confirmed by the physicist, La-beyrie, who joined us at that moment. Well, if the technicians said so, I was in for an uncomfortable time. Thank goodness I'd refused that second course. But why worry in advance? I put on a bold front and reached the bottom of the shake-hole, feeling like a gladiator in the arena. Other members of the team were waiting there to harness me and help me through the narrow entry to the shaft. This year I had given much thought to my wardrobe. A good deal of snow had fallen during the winter; the spring had been wet; and we anticipated that the cascade, which begins 722 feet below the surface, would be particularly heavy. Accordingly, I wore woollen underclothing and two suits of overalls, the first rub-berized and the outer one of stout canvas. Finally—an inno-vation which amused and intrigued the bystanders—I un-folded a large square of highly elastic sheet-rubber, in the centre of which I had cut a hole about the size of my fist. I passed my head through this hole, and was thus arrayed in a kind of *poncho* which covered me down to the waist and fitted close to my neck without strangling me.

The general effect, it seemed, was rather odd: the thing resembled a large white waterproof table-napkin, and made me look like an outsize baby about to eat its porridge! Pho-tographers came to snap me at close range, then stepped back a few paces so as not to impede my 'dressers.' As in 1953, it was Bidegain who helped me on with the heavy parachute harness; I was no more than a puppet in those powerful hands, which lifted me clean off the ground to make sure that the breast-strap was properly adjusted and would cause me no discomfort. Delteil busied himself with my helmet, inside which he adjusted the earphones. He inspected my breast-

lamp, and carefully fastened the mouth-piece on each side of
my neck. 'That's important,' he remarked; 'otherwise you
can't make yourself heard properly. I know, because I've got
a huge Adam's apple!'

And now Pierre Louis, attentive and methodical as ever,
was waiting for me at the entrance to the shaft. With ritual
precision he attached me to the end of the cable by means of
a climber's snap-hook. Henceforward I was linked to the
winding-gear and its attendants who waited only for a signal
to lower me.

I have already explained that the opening which gives immediate access to the shaft is so narrow and inconveniently
placed that you have to be something of an acrobat to get in
at all. Although one cannot go down Pierre Saint-Martin
without luggage, the kitbags which everyone carried slung
from each of the suspension straps were too bulky to pass
the opening in that position. One had therefore to slip
through oneself, and then wait on a narrow ledge 13 feet
down until the two bags were lowered on the end of a rope.

I had just entered and reached—13 when the sky above me
was darkened. I was surprised, and looked up. I could
scarcely believe my eyes. There was a perfectly colossal sack
being pushed through the hole. In due course it landed at
my side.

'Lévi,' I called up, 'I told you not to overload me; how do
you expect me to clean up the shaft with all this tied round
me?'

'I'm sorry,' he replied; 'but you'll have to forgive me. You
know the chasm as well as I do, and you know how I go to
work. One must be prepared for anything; you may be alone
down there for several days, and that bag contains only your
minimum requirements of tackle, food, and bedding.'

Another huge sack then arrived. Having to make the best
of it, I hooked on these two monstrosities which were to
weigh me down and prove a serious hindrance. Then I heard

a suave voice from on high: 'Maestro, you've forgotten one small item'; and there appeared a heavy 6 ft. 6 in. board. It was Lépineux who bade me this gracious farewell. Reluctantly I tied the thing to my belt so that it would hang below me, and was just going to call 'Lower away!' when someone else spoke. This time it was a photographer, leaning over the edge and asking me to 'look up and smile nicely!' One must try to oblige everyone, and above all not disappoint the Press. I therefore looked up; but I feel sure my smile was somewhat formal and contracted!

At last I was free to take off. I gave the signal, and had travelled rather less than 65 feet when I came to a halt. 'What's up?' I asked. 'Oh, nothing much,' Queffelec replied; 'but we shall have to ask you to be patient for a few minutes while we change the motor.'

Change the motor! I thought at first he was joking, but he assured me that it was unavoidable.

'How long will you be?'

'Oh, twenty minutes to half an hour. Will you stay where you are or come up again?'

Without those damned bags and the board I would have remained where I was, hanging in mid-air. As it was, I asked to come up, though much against my inclination; for it was quite a business in itself, nor is it good for morale to stay proceedings at the last moment and have to begin all over again. The job of passing out my baggage and then extricating myself, not to mention the intense heat of the shake-hole, caused me to perspire heavily in my woollens and waterproof overalls—an unfortunate circumstance, considering that I would soon have to plunge once more into the icy chasm.

Sitting on the ground, tired and roasting in my shell, I kept quite still in order not to aggravate the perspiration. Bidegain came up with a look of mingled concern and amusement. 'Well, Casteret,' he asked, 'are you going to spend your fifty-seventh birthday underground this year?' My birthday! Why of course; last year I had celebrated it (if I may use that phrase) in the chasm—I made a mental calculation and suddenly exclaimed: 'Good heavens, no! Don't suggest such a thing; there are twelve days to go.'

Half an hour later I was going down again quite normally and at a fair speed. Lépineux talked to me over the phone, ready with advice and encouragement until I reached the bottom.

Despite the weight of my baggage, I had to admit that I had been most skilfully harnessed; I was almost comfortable. Moreover, Robert Lévi, who is forever improving and perfecting, had substituted for the usual groin-straps and webbing of parachute harness a wooden seat and canvas back-strap. This was a distinct advantage; for whereas a parachute drop very rarely lasts more than a few minutes, our journeys might take several hours, during which the old equipment was liable to cause cramp, or at least a good deal of discomfort. Seated in the 'bosun's chair,' I arrived at—263, and was glad to find that Lépineux had thoroughly cleaned up the sloping balcony. I unfastened my talisman, the board, and fixed it in position with a few sharp hammer blows. There it would constitute a little barrier which would stop and hold further falls of stones. I stepped over it, hung in mid-air, and gave the word, 'Lower away!' But some 12 feet lower down I ran into trouble.

'Stop! Stop!' I called.

'What's the matter?'

'Nothing serious, but I'm stuck in a crevice,' I replied, making violent efforts to free myself.

'Casteret, you've lost your way,' said Lépineux who knew 'his' pot-hole by heart; 'you should have taken the right fork, not the left.'

'I know; but these blasted kitbags have dragged me off the path down here. Haul me up a couple of yards.'

That was better; I had managed to release myself, and descended without further mishap to—525 where the shaft is full of crevices, fissures, and small ledges piled with rubble which I swept down into the void as I passed by.

While thus engaged I witnessed a phenomenon which, though not uncommon, is most alarming, particularly in that situation. My headlamp suddenly revealed a lump of rock poised on a balcony that sloped inwards. It stood on a bed of sand and wet gravel. Was I . . . No, there was no illusion; the thing was moving. The inclination of the shelf, and the water trickling over it, had caused the gravel-bed to shift. It began cascading over the edge, followed almost immediately by the projectile itself, which must have weighed about 12 lb. Instinctively, but to no purpose here, since I was alone in the shaft, I shouted, 'Stone! Stone!' then smiled at my own nervousness as I heard the missile ricochet and break to pieces far below.

This episode recalled another incident that occurred here during the expedition of 1952, when five Lyons scouts and I went down on wire ladders, hoping to rescue Loubens. Fastened with *pitons* to the walls of rock at varying depths, we communicated with one another by word of mouth. Now the principal danger in course of these operations was falling stones dislodged by our own movements. Louis Ballandraux, who formed the spearhead, was frequently alarmed by the cry 'Pierre! Pierre!' It came from above, and warned him of an avalanche of rock. Crouched on the ladders, with his head well down between his shoulders, he trembled at what might be in store for him. After several of these alerts, he decided that there was no question of stones, but that someone was calling *Pierre* Epelly who was stationed about 300 feet or more above him. The lads subsequently agreed among themselves that in future Pierre Epelly should be known as Jules when thus engaged.

From this point the shaft was very damp; the walls oozed moisture, and whenever I touched them with bare hands, I received a slight but most unpleasant electric shock through my earphones. I learned afterwards that it was due to defective insulation, which was remedied by Rossini, our electrician. Thus tormented, I came at length to—699. At first I hardly knew where I was, so greatly had the place altered since last year.

If Lépineux had been surprised yesterday at—263, I was staggered now by the pile of debris on this next 'balcony.' With only a small geologist's hammer slung from my belt, I experienced a sense of frustration, helplessness. Besides, there were those accursed bags hanging at my sides; they tired and almost paralysed me. Each of them weighed quite 44 lb., and I began to wonder what on earth Lévi had stuffed them with. It seemed he had packed me off with provisions for a month!

Never mind; I had my job to do, and I must get on with it. No less than two hours were necessary to complete this exhausting labour. During that time I struggled with feet and hands to dislodge, lift, and throw down rocks and small stones. The pile seemed never to diminish, and I was obliged at intervals to stop work and lie down, panting, between my sacks. I guessed they were becoming impatient up above; the delay must have appeared interminable, and they might well be asking whether I should ever reach the bottom. Thanks, however, to a loudspeaker erected near the winch, everyone could hear those avalanches of stone which I unleashed, and which incidentally, were undermining my morale. It is not good to have to let loose repeated showers of rock inside a shaft, for they awaken the most dismal echoes which end by scaring even the most hardened explorer. As for the impatience of the surface team with those below, and *vice versa*, it is familiar to all speleologists.

Lépineux, who had spent more time in the chasm than on the surface, understood the difficulty of my task. He never lost his kindly calm.

'Hullo! Lépineux. I've had to stop for a few moments to get breath. I can't go on.'

'That's quite O.K. Take it easy; don't hurry,' he answered quietly.

At last, at the end of two hours' harassing toil, I was ready to resume my journey. My next ordeal would be the water-fall, and then that horrible spinning motion which Queffelec had predicted. From now onwards I would be suspended in mid-air at the end of a new steel cable which, so they said, was going to turn unceasingly. But I was so relieved to have completed the previous chore, and so eager to get to the bot-tom, that I was not greatly disturbed by the prospect of a cold douche and whirligig.

'Hullo, Lépineux, I'm just approaching the cascade.'

'Are you? Is it running strong?'

'No, it's extraordinary—a mere trickle.'

Yes, in spite of the heavy winter snows and a rainy spring, the cascade which had caused us so much discomfort on previous occasions, was insignificant. My beautiful rubber cape, thank heaven, was unnecessary! Of course I got wet; the water rattled on my helmet and shoulders, but nothing like so heavily as last year.

Lépineux asked me: 'By the way, are you spinning round?'

'Me? No, not at all.'

'Queffelec says you'll jolly soon be doing so.'

'Good, then I'll occupy myself counting the turns.'

As a matter of fact, on reaching the point where gyration formerly began, I started turning, but slowly, very slowly, then more slowly still—and it was over. I had counted only a few turns as against hundreds the year before. This new cable, which had been expected to twist so much, was very well designed and quite anti-gyratory. One should really not anticipate misfortune! And with that comforting thought I landed amid the huge boulders of the Salle Lépineux.

'Thanks, Queffelec, you've got me here in an armchair!'

The journey had taken me exactly three hours, and I was all in. I stumbled a few paces down to the bivouac, where I was at last able to relieve myself of my two bags and harness, and to exchange the ponderous flying helmet for my usual tin hat. I had entered again into possession of these halls which I had left twelve months ago.

At the foot of an enormous rock 65 feet high and 100 long, I found our reserve of tinned foods, calcium carbide, various accessories, and a few oddments. Nothing had changed, all was just the same as if we had been here a few days before. There was also a roll of telephone-wire; and I now attached one end of it to the terminal buckle of the cable, which would henceforward be in almost continual motion between the Salle Lépineux and the surface. These journeys necessitated constant vigilance. Members of the team were for the most part lowered and brought up without a hitch; but in past years we had had a deal of trouble with the loose cable owing to friction and fouling, and to prevent these delays we had to keep it taut. I was doing that now, paying out the wire a little at a time as the cable rose, and holding it straight.

While the cable was being wound up, my telephone was out of use; but as soon as that operation was finished I could unpack an instrument from my kitbag and connect it to the wire. Alas! Last year's mishap was repeated. I was carefully unrolling the wire, like an angler paying out his line, when I felt it go limp in my hand. That well-known whistling sound gave warning, and pierced me to the heart. The wire, of course, had broken; it fell at my feet looking like a tangled wig.

I was now cut off altogether. I wondered, too, whether the cable was continuing its upward journey, or was jammed somewhere in a crevice. I should have to kick my heels until the next man arrived; and he might be delayed for a host of reasons. All I knew was that my first companion would be Robert Lévi, than whom it would have been impossible to find a more strenuous and conscientious leader. He had insisted on coming down to consider the difficulties of exhumation, to take part in it, and to assess the problem of raising the container.

For want of something better to do, I started to unpack my kitbags, and was immediately grateful for Lévi's solicitude and experience. There was a butane gas stove, a thermix heater, a telephone instrument (at the moment useless), and a heap of foodstuffs ('iron rations'). . . . Suddenly I dropped everything and made a dive for the wall. I had caught sight of a magnificent amber-coloured beetle; it was scared, and moved rapidly, but I caught it in a matchbox. Not being an entomologist, I had none of the correct glass tubes. But lying on the ground was a used bottle of excellent Martinique punch left over from last year. Sufficient liquid remained in which to drown the insect. It was a splendid specimen of the extremely rare *Aphaenops Loubensi* which Prof. Jeannel of the Musée de Paris had classified in 1953 as a new species.

The disposal of my luggage and the capture of the insect was not enough to occupy my leisured solitude, so I decided to relax for a quarter of an hour and take a rest. I was suffering from fatigue and nervous tension, but the effect of stretching myself out on the floor was opposite to that which I expected. I became more than ever on edge; besides, the low temperature and dampness of the chasm is intolerable unless one keeps moving about. I got up and walked down to the tomb, and from there went on to the site of last year's camp. The same bits and pieces lay scattered about; a battered helmet, a torn mattress, some empty tins, etc. . . . It was all very dreary; so I climbed back to the bivouac, stopping for a moment and holding my breath to listen for a voice or a falling stone in the great shaft. Nothing moved. I then decided to fill in time with a meal . . . Some lumps of rock came whistling down, and I ducked behind a large boulder. A mouthful of food had given me new heart, and those flying fragments told me that someone was coming down. It was 6 p.m.; I waited anxiously for the least sound, and felt glad that Lévi would soon land at my side.

But at midnight I was still waiting, and asked myself for the hundredth time that inevitable question: 'What the hell are they doing up there?'

In desperation, I put on an extra sweater under my overalls, lay down on a slab of rock, extinguished my lamp, and tried to sleep. Lévi's descent must have been postponed for some good reason until tomorrow.

At 2 a.m., as I tossed and turned on my rocky bed, there was a feeble cry far up in the shaft. Half an hour later Robert Lévi touched down. At last! I had been expecting him for fifteen hours, and had almost given up hope. He told me that he had been delayed time after time, but had determined to get down, no matter what the cost.

Sunday, 8th August. Returning to the bivouac at about 9 a.m., we were able to phone the surface; for the cable had not been wound up again since Lévi's arrival. When the time came for its departure, we again unrolled the guidewire. Again it broke, leaving us in isolation!

We were resigned to our situation, hoping the cable would reach its destination before long, and certain of our programme. Delteil was to come down next; he had volunteered for the delicate and unpleasant task of bringing down the metal coffin. . . .

At about 8 o'clock that evening a small avalanche of stones informed us of Delteil's approach.

Flushed with excitement after his memorable journey, Delteil was magnificent. He had battled all alone in the great shaft for three hours, and looked like a *poilu* at Verdun, with feverish eyes, his face lined with fatigue, his harness in disorder, his overalls torn, and one of his hands bleeding.

Our next job was to bear the coffin to the tomb. After

slipping and stumbling from top to bottom of the slope, we
got it into position ready for the exhumation, which was to
take place as soon as we were joined by Dr. Mairey and Louis
Ballandraux, who would not be down until tomorrow. It was
now 11 p.m. We had done enough for one day, and therefore
withdrew, dead-beat, to a little tent which was scarcely large
enough for three. Although packed like sardines, we were
soon fast asleep.

Monday, 9th August. I awoke with a feeling that it was
time to get up, and took a peep at my companions. Delteil,
as usual, was snoring hard; but Lévi, to judge by his breathing, was awake.

'Lévi, what's the time?' I whispered, switching on my torch
discreetly veiled in a handkerchief.

My neighbour stretched himself, looked at his wrist watch,
and then put it sharply to his ear. 'It says 11 o'clock, but it's
not going,' he replied. 'It must have stopped last evening.'

I had left my watch in a suit of overalls that were in my
haversack, and this lay some distance from the tent which
was too small to hold anything but us three. Having extricated myself from my sleeping bag, I crawled out of the
tent, pulled on my boots, and eventually retrieved my watch.
Good heavens! . . . yes; the second-hand was moving, so
the thing had definitely not stopped.

'Guess,' I said to Lévi.

'It's at least 8 o'clock in the morning,' he answered.

'Don't be absurd,' protested Delteil, who had just woken
up. 'It's the dead of night!'

'Dead dark, certainly,' I rejoined, 'but believe me or not,
it's midday!'

Neither of them would believe me at first; they thought
I was joking. But it was a fact; down there in the chasm,
where the temperature was no more than 39° Fahrenheit and
the humidity 100 per cent, we had slept fully-clothed in a

tiny tent for thirteen hours! None of us had ever done anything like it, and we fell to discussing so memorable a feat.
We were cut short by a formidable shower of stones.

'Hark! there's someone on the stairs,' said Lévi quietly.
'Another bloke dropping in for lunch,' added Delteil.

We hurried immediately to the bivouac, where Louis Ballandraux had just touched down, carrying two outsize kitbags in addition to his normal load.

During the afternoon we were joined by Doctor Mairey,
who brought his medicine chest, several pairs of rubber
gloves, and various accessories. We now prepared to carry
out the work of exhumation, and were shortly afterwards
gathered at the tomb. In that unstable mass of rock, it took
us several hours to construct a horizontal platform on which
to lay the container and walk about.

There were only four pairs of gloves; so it was agreed that
Delteil, who had badly lacerated hands, should be excused
from touching the body. At 6 p.m. we began demolishing,
stone by stone, the great tumulus beneath which Marcel had
been lying for two years, arrayed, as he had fallen, like a
medieval knight. He wore his helmet, and, in place of the
sword, a torch lay on his breast.

At 9 p.m., exhausted with fatigue and emotion, we removed our gloves. Delteil screwed down the lid, and we put
forth what was left of our strength and determination to drag
the heavy coffin to a point immediately below the shaft
where in due course it could be attached to the end of the
cable.

We had fulfilled our task, and it was now the turn of those
who were to prepare the shaft for the container's upward
journey. Lépineux and Bidegain went down to −263, La-
beyrie and Rossini to −699. It had been calculated that their
job would take two days.

The preparation of the balconies consisted in erecting near
the rim of each a metal lattice girder 6 feet 6 inches long.
These were meant to steer the container clear of overhangs,

and thus avoid it becoming hung up or jammed in a crevice—events which might prove dangerous if not disastrous. Each girder was made of duralumin sections (another of Lépineux's ideas), and was fitted at its base with a spindle enabling it to swing from side to side, and at the opposite end with a stout wooden pulley to facilitate the cable's passage. Numerous stays, carefully placed and tightly stretched, assured the firmness and rigidity of the girder. Driving *pitons* into the rocky walls, in situations no less perilous than inconvenient, was a job whose difficulty was increased by the fact that our men were obliged to work beneath small but icy-cold cascades, consequent upon a series of violent storms which had transformed the shaft into an aqueduct. It was even necessary on several occasions to interrupt the work and hurriedly bring up the teams—for fear of lightning, which is attracted by pot-holes. The long steel cable hanging in the shaft would prove a dangerous conductor. On the evening of the exhumation, after pitching a tent for Mairey and Ballandraux, we were roused from sleep at about midnight by the roll of thunder which grew minute by minute; and the cascade in the shaft, swollen by an exceptionally heavy downpour, allowed us a glimpse of its awful possibilities. At the same time, another sound, even more alarming, rose from the depths. This was the subterranean torrent in flood, growling below the chaos of rock. Hence the internal changes of the chasm—those traces of extensive flooding which we observed last year, and the collapse of boulders. The whole place roared, vibrated, and there were falls of stone. Pierre Saint-Martin was in labour; we were in a living chasm in full process of evolution.

Lying in absolute darkness, wrapped in our sleeping bags under the frail and illusory shelter of our canvas tents, the consciousness of our weak and helpless state in presence of this awful demonstration taught us an eloquent lesson of humility.

All things considered, we were lucky to escape with nothing worse than a restless night. Mairey and Ballandraux were in worse danger than the rest; for their tent was pitched on a stretch of gravel, clearly the bed of a river which might at any moment have reappeared but was, in fact, absorbed by its own deposit before reaching our camp.

Tuesday, 10th August. At 9 a.m. I went up to the bivouac with Louis Ballandraux who had brought down a wireless transmitter and was anxious to establish communication with the surface, for the telephone was still cut off. He managed to converse with Fr. Attout, thanks largely to the cable, which had been lowered to −699 and served as a conductor for the waves between that point and the outside world. Among other things, we learned that Mauer would be joining us later in the day. He landed at noon, carrying another two kitbags and a large roll of telephone-wire. Lévi, as chief of the expedition, was now required on the surface; he went up trailing this after him, and we looked forward to re-establishing contact with those above.

In the normal course of events three more of us would have followed Lévi without further delay; only two men would be needed to attach the coffin to the cable and assist at its take-off when the moment arrived. As it was, however, we had other plans.

We had been categorically forbidden to do any more exploring, and were supposed to limit our activities to recovering Loubens's body. From the very start we had considered these instructions as an unjustifiable abuse of authority; we had signed no undertaking, and it was therefore with an easy conscience that I decided upon my own responsibility to ignore them.

The finding of this pot-hole had been the climax of a search begun by E. A. Martel in 1908, and continued at intervals between 1925 and 1950 by the Groupe Spéléologique de la Pierre Saint-Martin led by Max Cosyns and myself. Lépineux had actually made the discovery; Loubens, another member of the group, had died here; and Dr. Mairey had been the victim of what might easily have been a fatal accident. So Pierre Saint-Martin was in a very real sense 'ours,' and to go home without trying to explore upstream would have been a miserable surrender of our rights. In any case, we could not have restrained the determination of fellows like Mairey, Mauer, and Ballandraux. Besides, to finish the job was surely the noblest honour we could render to poor Loubens's memory.

A party set out at 4 o'clock in the afternoon; it consisted of Mairey, Ballandraux and Mauer. I stayed behind with Delteil, one of whose hands had been badly lacerated.

I had no fears as I watched the other three disappear from sight. All were highly trained and well-tried speleologists.

Our companions had been gone an hour when I climbed that mass of cyclopean boulders in the Salle Lépineux which they had now left behind, and through which Mairey and I had begun our journey upstream (due south into Spanish territory) twelve months ago. My immediate purpose was to revisit a platform of rock where I knew there was a colony of diptera, a kind of mosquito. Lost in this immensity, they had for some unknown cause, taken up residence just here, where I soon found them. Isolated from one another, and quite motionless, they look so easy to catch; but as soon as you approach with a light, they scurry sideways over the rock—like crabs. When they become conscious of imminent danger, they take to flight; and then you begin to appreciate their unwillingness to use their wings. They are poor flyers with an uncertain, dipping movement; and they soon come to rest on the floor or on another rock, but always below their starting-point. Their clumsy flight is due, of course, to atrophy of the wings consequent upon their surroundings; and I have no doubt that in another few thousand years these

strange mosquitoes of Pierre Saint-Martin will be wingless.
The few that I caught were destined for the microscopes in
the Musée de Paris.

During my stroll I came across a short strip of Scotch-light,
a piece of cloth treated with reflecting material in the form
of powdered catadioptric glass. It was a guide-mark left by
Mairey and his companions. These objects, when strategi-
cally placed, enable one to go ahead without fear of losing
one's way on the return journey through the complicated
maze of debris. I followed the trail of these guideposts until
I heard the voices of my friends. They were looking for a
road to the head-waters, but repeatedly found their passage
blocked by boulders reaching to the ceiling. I felt certain, as
they did, that once they had overcome these difficulties, and
pierced some gap in the wall, they would find the chasm extended for some considerable distance.

I returned to the bivouac. Delteil was busy patching his
overalls; they had suffered badly during his descent with the
container and were actually in rags. We employ somewhat
original tailoring methods at Pierre Saint-Martin; holes are
made in the material with the point of a knife, and telephone
wire takes the place of thread. While Delteil was thus engaged I sat on the ground beside him and made a few entries
in my note-book. Suddenly we heard a noise high up in the
shaft, as of someone falling. It grew louder; and as we
ducked, a body landed with a terrifying crash at a distance
of 13 or 14 feet on the debris slope. From there it rolled out
of sight. Horror-struck and trembling, we jumped up and
hurried down to find the unhappy man who had just been
killed before our very eyes. Delteil pulled up sharply and
bent over a contorted mass. Then he stood erect with a shout
of laughter. Thank God! The victim of that dreadful fall was
only a large kitbag which had escaped from its owner at—
699 and fallen 436 feet to the bottom. It had burst open, and
we picked up a number of articles, including a camera

(which as you may guess, was useless). We knew then that the bag belonged to Vergnes. Having recovered from the shock, we resumed our peaceful if trivial occupations.

Presently Robert Vergnes himself came down and joined us. His arrival was far more sedate than that of his kitbag. Mairey, Mauer and Ballandraux returned soon afterwards, pleased with their reconnaissance and tremendously excited. They had managed with some difficulty to pass the danger zone, where rocks and ceiling met, and found, as I had predicted, that the gigantic wilderness of rock extended much farther.

Our commandos had done a fine job, and had turned back in order to make their report. I was thrilled, and determined to lead a party on the following day as far as it was possible to go.

Wednesday, 11th August. This was to be the day of days —if one may speak of 'day' in places where there is no dawn. It would provide an answer to that question we had left unanswered for a year: did the chasm reach into Spanish territory; and if so, how far?

Pierre Saint-Martin consists of a shaft, 1,135 feet deep, giving access to an enormous cavity through which flows a subterranean river. In 1953 we had travelled down-stream for a distance of nearly two miles and to a depth of 2,389 feet in French territory. How far would we get today, through the chaos of its head-waters, into Spain?

The whole team, excepting Vergnes and Delteil, set off at 8 a.m. We expected to be absent for at least a day, perhaps two if all went well. On leaving the bivouac we had to climb in heavy kit up that mountain of boulders, which stands at the near end of the Salle Lépineux, and then descend the opposite face, guided by Scotch-lights which Mairey had laid yesterday. Presently the doctor pointed out one of these signposts lying on a rock which was not on our present track.

It was of a pattern used last year, and I recognized it as marking the spot where he and I had forced our way into the heart of the wilderness.

Mairey smiled as we passed that Scotch-light which had so nearly marked the end of his career as a speleologist; and before long we reached the summit of a rise which we had to descend with the help of an electron ladder. This manœuvre brought us out from the labyrinth into a colossal chamber, so vast and tortuous that we could make out neither its size nor its shape. It was perfectly stupendous, exceeding all conceivable dimensions, far transcending human architecture.

'Since we are now in Spain,' I said, 'let us call this prodigious chamber "Salle de Navarre"; territorially the name is correct, and it will be a gesture towards our Spanish friends who had hoped to be with us on this occasion.'

I have travelled a good deal in Spain, especially in the mountainous province of Navarre; but I can safely say that I have never seen in the whole of the Peninsula so wild a stretch of country as that through which we now advanced by lamp-light. Here Earth's structure, which so fascinates Delteil, is set forth on the grandest scale. The journey became so arduous and complicated that we had to make alternate use of ropes and wire ladders in order to negotiate precipice-roads or steep cliffs.

Mauer was lagging behind when he suddenly called for help. We turned round and saw him kneeling, apparently in difficulties on the sloping ground. But there was nothing wrong; he was interested in something quite different from the recovery of his balance. Considering this fearful desert of rock, his eyesight was most remarkable, for he had noticed an insect—a superb *Aphaenops Loubensi* which Mairey recognized as a giant of the species. Taking from his entomologist's pack a small wet paint-brush, he caught the beetle, and put it in a tube of alcohol. It was the fifth specimen to fall into our hands in two years. Animal life, of course, does not abound here; conditions are too severe to make existence anything but precarious.

We should really have been gaining height, since we were travelling upstream. In point of fact, however, we had spent most of our time going downhill. Ballandraux was walking ahead; or rather he was tumbling and jumping from rock to rock, for the ground seemed to consist mainly of pits, fissures and crevasses. He had just made a neat landing on top of a great tubular rock, when we realized with horror that the thing had begun to swing forwards. Then, as in a dream, we saw Ballandraux raised higher and higher into the air. Here was an example of those swaying boulders known as 'Crazy Stones.'

Having recovered from his surprise, Ballandraux purposely renewed the see-saw movement, the effect of which was amplified by the height and mass of the rock. We called it 'Roche Ballandraux,' and each enjoyed a spell of its majestic oscillation.

We might also have exercised the privilege of pioneers and named the huge gallery through which we now proceeded over jagged ground. Our attention, however, was riveted upon the difficulties of progress and of finding our direction, so that we had neither the leisure nor the freedom of imagination to assign names and titles to the places through which we passed.

At this point the torrent flows quite close to the surface, but is still hidden by great boulders beneath which you can hear it rumbling. We were already moving uphill; but the way before us involved an exhausting climb to the level of the ceiling, so we decided to call a halt and have some lunch. Nearby was a small cascade issuing from the wall; it was a tributary of the main stream, but with a temperature of 39° Fahrenheit it was not much use for diluting the concentrated milk, of which Mairey had produced several tubes from his haversack. I proceeded to distribute pieces of sausage, which Ballandraux cut into rounds with the blade of a metal saw. Having no bread, we rounded off our meal with two packets of dry cake, and then moved on. Presently my companions led me into a narrow passage, on the ceiling of which there were numerous stalactites which did not greatly impress me. I told them so quite frankly; they were shocked, and put me down as blasé!

Yesterday's journey had ended at this point. But the system extended farther in undiminished grandeur; the way continued rough and downhill. We now separated, and each took a different path in order to check up on and eliminate blind alleys. After several reconnaissances and a brief council of war at the rallying point, it was clear that Mauer had found the right track. We followed him over some very rough ground into a winding corridor where we found the river. We advanced first on one bank and then on the other, sometimes on natural bridges and perilous overhangs. It was a strenuous and exciting journey, and we longed to know where it would lead us. At every bend, at every barrier of rock, we quickened our pace to seek what might lie beyond, and to assure ourselves that yet more distant perspectives opened out beneath those mysterious vaults. So far, however, we had kept our heads. The obstacle which now met our gaze was enough to daunt the bravest of the brave.

We had been walking for some minutes on banks that narrowed steadily above foaming rapids. Suddenly the river became deep, and flowed between vertical walls of smooth rock. We could go no farther, except by swimming in that icy water at a temperature of about 37° F., sufficient to cool the most determined hot-head! We had no collapsible boat, not even a raft; but we managed to balance ourselves on an isthmus of rock, which enabled us to advance a few yards and ascertain that 40 or 50 feet beyond that point the stream made a right-angled bend; its far bank was a sheer wall of

stone. Considering its enormous width elsewhere, this sec-
tion of the gallery was relatively small—16 or 20 feet wide
by about 13 feet in height. The contraction set up a violent
current of cold air, a regular hurricane, which pierced us to
the bone, extinguished our lamps, and churned the surface
of the water. This wind, blowing at gale force, proves that
the cavern extends for a great distance upstream; but the
depth of the river constitutes an impassable barrier unless
one has means of navigation. We had come as far as would
be possible this year.

We had already started to retrace our steps, when I caught
sight of a corridor running upstream and parallel with the
river. I hurried in, hoping against hope that it might by-pass
the deep water; but after walking for about 55 yards, I found
that the ceiling came down to meet the floor while the walls
huddled closer together. 'It's a cul-de-sac! There's no road
here,' I shouted back to my companions who were ferreting
about in a maze of secondary passages.

'Casteret! Come and look. Here are some wonderful stalactites.'

It was Mairey's voice. Stalactites! Fancy thinking about
stalactites when we had just been brought to a halt in the
most incredible cavern I had ever seen! Sadly, I turned
back, conquered by deep water on one side and by a cul-de-
sac on the other. My three companions, on the other hand,
seemed already to have forgotten their disappointment; they
were talking excitedly and admiring their 'wonderful stalactites.'

'Casteret, do come here,' Mairey insisted, 'and tell us what
you think of them.' I rejoined them, feeling not a little
sceptical; in fact, I was in no mood to share their enthusiasm.
But on raising my eyes to the ceiling, I quickly changed my
tune: 'Good for you!' I cried, 'they're magnificent, extraordinary.' It is impossible to describe an outcrop of helictites;
perfection is always indescribable. But as an expert crystal-

lographer, who has visited more than one thousand caves, I unhesitatingly award the prize for rarity and delicacy to the stalactites of Pierre Saint-Martin.

It was growing late. We cast a final glance at the helictites, a final glance too at the deep water, and resumed our journey. At one stage Ballandraux, having unpacked his drawing-pad, compasses, and pencil proceeded to map the chasm. Mairey and Mauer went ahead with the lamp upon which our surveyor based his readings. I stayed behind for the time being to give him light and a helping hand in awkward places. Between the four of us we worked out approximate distances and contours. Our reckoning was probably not far out, especially as sights were for the most part fairly short.

Our journey through the Salle de Navarre gave rise to some differences of opinion as to its real dimensions. In order to clear the matter up, I undertook a solitary excursion which led me over ridges of rock, gigantic crags, and 'Crazy Stones' that seemed ready to crash down at any moment. Finally, I lost myself in a veritable labyrinth of boulders, the end of which I could not see; and it was some time before I succeeded in rejoining my companions, who, in spite of the Scotch-lights, had resorted once again to hair-raising feats of acrobatics in order to escape from the labyrinth.

We returned to the bivouac at 6 p.m. after a forced march and a regular display of acrobatics. It had taken us eight hours to cover the 1¼ miles there and back, which should give some idea of the difficulties involved. The cavern extended for 1,100 yards into Spanish territory; and that distance added to two miles on the French side, gives a 4,620 yard stretch of uninterrupted chaos so far explored.

Delteil and Vergnes, who had anxiously awaited the result of our expedition, informed us that work in the shaft was more or less up to schedule, although it was proving a most delicate and awkward business. It seemed then, that the entire chasm had been a hive of activity. We sat around the oven and chatted while our one hot meal of the day was cooking.

But our joy and satisfaction was tempered by the presence of the coffin which shone through the gloom. It had never ceased to dominate our thoughts.

Thursday, 12th August. Early this morning there was much ado in the tent occupied by Mairey, Mauer, and Ballandraux. They rose, dressed, trimmed their acetylene lamps, drew their rations, and prepared to set off. The three of them were going to revisit the bottom of the chasm, which some of us had reached in 1953. Dr. Mairey, who had formed one of the party on that occasion, and was therefore acquainted with the road, would take charge now. The newcomers, Mauer and Ballandraux, had been longing to make the journey; but this was to be more than just a pleasure-trip, and before they started I ran over the subjects upon which they were to make notes: topography, temperature, humidity, air currents, barometric pressure, and biology. They were also to take photographs.

Vergnes was bitterly disappointed that he was not going with them; but his camera was out of action, so he could do nothing in the way of making film. He was to return to the surface some time this morning. The cable would soon be lowered, for we had been informed by telephone that someone else was coming down to join us. He arrived an hour later, and Vergnes went up almost immediately. Our visitor was Fr. Jacques Attout, who with Lorian of Charleroi formed the Belgian element which we always included in our Group. He confirmed Delteil's news that preparation of the balconies was well advanced in spite of difficulties. Numerous *pitons* were required to secure the girders; but storms on the surface were delaying work, which had frequently to be broken off. This year's campaign had been inaugurated under the sign of foul weather.

Fr. Attout and I traversed the Salle Lépineux from end to end and from side to side. Looking down into the shaft which gives access to the Salle Elizabeth Casteret, we saw a wire ladder; Mairey, Mauer and Ballandraux had fixed it there earlier in the day. An icy wind howled ceaselessly in this place, and was no encouragement to stay for long; so we returned to the bivouac where Delteil mounted solitary guard at the telephone.

'Father, there's a message for you,' he said as we approached.

'What about?'

'Your bishop has appointed you parish priest of some out-of-the-way place—I've forgotten its name.'

It was perfectly true; so you see the Pierre Saint-Martin telephone had its uses—when it worked!

At about 7 p.m. Fr. Attout unpacked a small case containing his priestly vestments, an altar stone, a chalice and other necessities for the celebration of mass. The altar was an irregular slab of rock. The servers wedged themselves uncomfortably between a vertical wall and a heap of boulders; Delteil lit the two small candles, and I laid the tiny cruets at my feet. Over his alb, etc. the priest donned a beautiful white chasuble with green orphreys; it was almost startling amid that wild, dark scenery. But if the altar was a wretched makeshift affair, and if we ourselves were ragged, dirty, and unshaven after a week underground, 'it is the spirit that quickeneth.'

The celebrant told us that he was going to offer the Holy Sacrifice for the repose of Marcel Loubens's soul and for the success of the dangerous undertaking to which we had pledged ourselves. Mass then began, the coffin lying only a few feet from the altar.

An hour later Mairey's team came back, haggard and exhausted, but flushed with success. They had carried out their programme in full: having crossed the seven huge chambers and travelled more than 3 miles through an unimaginable chaos, they had reached the bottom of the cavern where the altimeter confirmed last year's reading of 2,389 feet.

Friday, 13th August. I spent a restless night. At midnight and 1 a.m. Bidegain phoned to keep me informed of progress. At 2 o'clock he told me that work on the balconies was complete. Between then and 6 a.m. the men responsible for this achievement were raised to the surface. It was now the turn of those at the bottom, excepting two who were to attach the container to the cable and guide it past the great boulders of the Salle Lépineux after the take-off.

We had much difficulty with the cable on its downward journey, in spite of the guide-wire which was handled from below. Over and over again it became entangled on projections of rock, and had to be pulled this way and that before it was freed. At long last, however, it was in position, and I prepared to leave the cavern.

I had spent hours of alternate joy and sorrow, but one decision had yet to be made: what to do with a small crucifix hanging on the wall. On 13th August, 1952, as Marcel lay dying at the bottom of the shaft, Father Atauri, a Spanish priest from San Sebastian who was among a crowd of spectators on the surface, had detached this cross from his rosary and asked Dr. Mairey to lay it on the stretcher. Mairey had in fact nailed it to the wall nearby, and it had hung there ever since—a lonely symbol in the waste of that tremendous chasm. I was aware that it belonged to a rosary given to Fr. Atauri by his mother and of great sentimental value in his eyes, so I took it down and slipped it into my pocket-book.

At 2 o'clock in the afternoon I linked the snap-hook of my harness to the cable, gave the signal by telephone, and felt

myself raised from the ground, turning, swaying in mid-air.
On this my seventh consecutive day underground, I had
reason to feel satisfied; but I was distinctly off-colour after
that long sojourn in a cold, damp atmosphere, during which
my diet had been, to say the least, unorthodox. Lack of sunlight, on the other hand, which is often supposed to cause
lassitude and even claustrophobia, had had no ill effects. My
eyesight had, if anything, improved; I had the vision of a cat
by night.

Within fifty minutes I was out of the shaft, standing in
bright sunshine beneath an azure sky. Willing hands stripped
me of my harness; I climbed those last few yards of rope-
ladder, and sat down by the winding-gear. Queffelec was
still at the helm, cheerful, confident, and bold as brass.
Nearby was a party of girls dressed in shorts, members of a
holiday-camp, who eyed me with unfeigned curiosity from
top to toe. Unwashed, unshaven, my drawn face smeared
with clay, and overalls in shreds, I must have seemed to them
a miserable specimen of humanity. Questions crowded one
upon another, but I have only the haziest recollection of
that half-hour.

I then strolled up to the camp, and was greeted at the
cookhouse by Henri Périllous, who gave me the first proper
meal I had been able to enjoy since entering the chasm. I
returned to the winch and saw Henri Brosset go down to
help Ballandraux attach the coffin. Delteil was then hauled to
the surface, followed by Mairey. Father Attout was delayed
by a tremendous storm which obliged us to postpone operations until next day.

Saturday, 14th August. Fr. Attout came up at 6 a.m. during a hailstorm and in dense fog. Mauer was then hauled to
the balcony at −699; Lépineux and Bidegain went down to
join him.

This was Judgement-day, to which we had looked forward

with hope and yet with dread. My thoughts were with Lépineux, Mauer, and Bidegain making their last inspection of the gear. Queffelec adjusted his engine and the winch. It was almost zero hour. Lévi, wearing earphones, spoke hurriedly with the lads at −699, and then with the Salle Lépineux. Labeyrie crouched over the radio, ready to take over if the telephone should fail. Ballandraux and Brosset had just attached the cable to the head of the container, and the girder at −699 was in position. The stage was set.

At exactly 5 p.m. Lévi passed Lépineux's signal to the engineers, and Queffelec threw his engine into gear. The rise of tension was alarming; the machinery vibrated and slipped the dynamometer showed 1,100 lb. But the container was off the ground, clear of the huge boulders, and was rising slowly. Every available member of the party stood by, as well as a few journalists. There were about fifteen of us all told, huddling together round the winch beneath the shelter of a canvas awning, while rain and hail poured down in torrents, driven by great gusts of wind. In spite of the weather, our attention was concentrated entirely upon the dynamometer and upon the cable as it wound slowly on the drum. We dared not speak. All eyes turned towards Queffelec whose smile had given place to a grim and anxious look. Gradually, however, he relaxed; his countenance cleared, and he gave his assistant Isola a friendly pat on the back.

'Well, it's coming up all right,' he said.

Yes, it was coming up all right. Progress was slow and painful; but it was progress, and our faces showed a lessening of fear.

We had regarded this phase of the journey as most critical; the initial haul had counted for so much, and the container had seemed at that moment so very far away. On second thoughts, however, the situation appeared different. Until now the manœuvre had involved no danger of contact with the walls. . . . The dynamometer jerked several times and startled us.

'It's nothing,' said Lévi. 'It's bumping against the wall every now and again, but there's worse than that to come.'

Holding the receiver of his telephone to the loudspeaker, he enabled us to hear the dismal sound of the container; it resembled a cracked bell. He spoke again into the mouthpiece:

'Approaching −699. Hullo, Lépineux! Let me know as soon as you catch sight of it.'

'I see nothing yet; there's that sea of cloud below us . . . Oh yes! Here it comes, like a ghost out of the mist.'

There was a dull, heavy sound; the container was in contact with the girder, and a few seconds later it had cleared that dangerous overhang. Lépineux and Mauer had had some anxious moments. One of the *pitons* had come loose; the girder had leaned over, and they had to use all their strength to avoid an accident and, perhaps, disaster.

The container was now dragged on to the balcony and made fast while Lépineux unhooked the cable and attached it to his own harness. Bidegain followed; they were going up to −263 to help with the remainder of the operation. Mauer was to remain alone at −699 and re-attach the container as soon as the cable had been lowered. His situation was fraught with peril. If there were a fall of stones, if the cable snapped, or if some other untoward incident occurred, he would be in the direct line of fire.

Lépineux had joined Bidegain and Rossini at −263 and together they made final preparations for the arrival and reception of the container. On the surface, bad weather continued unabated; we were drenched to the skin and buffeted by an icy gale. The Spanish *carabiniers*, of their charity and unasked, brought us great logs of dead pine wood. They managed also to light a brazier which bore us company throughout that night.

All subterranean work is terribly slow and complicated, and it was some time before the cable was lowered again and Mauer attached it to the nose of the container. Fortunately the telephone was working well; all messages were passed and repeated between −699, −263, and the winch. The next stage of the journey could begin. But just as Lévi was about to give Queffelec the signal, I motioned him to wait. I had glanced at the clock on the instrument board: it was precisely 10 p.m. 'Two years ago today at this very hour,' I said, 'Marcel died. Let's pause for a few moments.' Lévi nodded assent and passed my message to those underground. The whole party observed a minute's silence, drawing from the recollection of that tragedy in 1952 a stern resolve to succeed in their present task. Those of us on the surface were little more than passive, helpless spectators of the drama which now approached its climax.

Mauer had bidden farewell to the container. He was alone now at −699 where he was doomed to remain and suffer through long hours. Lépineux shall now take up the tale. Crouched with José Bidegain and Rossini at −263, he had checked up on the girder.

'The cable was rising; our eyes were glued to the pulley. "It must be getting close now, José," I remarked. "We shan't have long to wait." Rossini phoned the surface to ask for position. Queffelec answered that the container was at −525. At that critical point there was an angle of rock under which it might easily become jammed, and we began to have serious misgivings about the next stage of the journey.

'Almost immediately we were startled by a loud noise, and the cable stopped vibrating. Rossini snatched the telephone. . . . The winch had ceased to turn, and the dynamometer had risen from 880 to 2,200 lb. Three times I had the container lowered and raised; three times it jammed, making a tremendous din. Lévi's voice held a note of grave anxiety: "What do you propose doing?" José and I looked at one an-

other. Then I said: "Eat and think. We've got to take our
time over this. How late is it?" "Nearly midnight," Lévi
replied.

Sunday, 15th August. The crisis was upon us. The wind
howled unceasingly, and rain gave place to heavy snow
which froze us to the marrow. A journalist, crouching at my
side, leaned over and said: 'Nature has unleashed all her
forces; the storm, the mountain and the chasm are allied
against you. It seems as if the malignant spirits of the place
refuse to yield up their prey and Loubens back to you.'

It was clear to those underground, as it was to us gathered
round the winch, that there was only one thing to be done:
the auto-hoist was a last resource whose use had been fore-
seen as possible, although we had entertained secret hopes
that it would not prove necessary. This appliance was de-
vised by Queffelec. It was a sort of pulley-block, hanging
from which a man could raise or lower himself by hand along
a steel-wire cable—rather like a plasterer on the façade of a
building. It had been very seldom used by speleologists, and
requires special training. Before this expedition, Bidegain,
Lépineux, and I had agreed to practice with it in a small
chasm and so familiarize ourselves with its use. As things
turned out I had not been able to take part in these exercises
on account of a fall while climbing. Lépineux had been
obliged therefore to act as Bidegain's assistant; hence no one
but José had so far used the apparatus, which requires a good
deal of practice. As a precaution, all this gear had been stored
on the balcony at −263. Here, then, Lépineux drove in ex-
panding *pitons* to which the cable of the hoist was to be
fixed. Bidegain now made himself fast, and his two companions watched him sink slowly out of sight.

Thanks be to God, the only member of the team qualified
to use the hoist was a man of calm courage and herculean
strength. He alone could have accomplished that over-

whelming task. The lot had fallen upon him; he accepted it, and carried it out at the peril of his life and to the limit of physical endurance.

Having reached the container, he would have to release it and escort it on its way, hauling himself up meanwhile yard by yard, hugging the thing to himself and never letting go. I will let him tell the tale; his words far surpass any that I could write.

'On my way down I was haunted by one fear: would the great cable cross my slender thread, squeeze it against a rock, and cut it through? If that happened, there could be no hope: I must inevitably hurtle into space. I recalled Casteret's grave warning as he returned to the surface: "It is going to be a very dangerous operation . . . and I know what I'm talking about." However, I arrived safely at my destination, level with the coffin wedged beneath that cursed overhang. After some manœuvering, which I directed by telephone, I succeeded in placing it in the position from which I judged it easiest to pass the ledge. Now for it: "Up!"

'With my back to the wall, pushing the massive weight with hands and feet, I got it past the obstacle. It was crushing me, but it was going up. Foot by foot we rose together.'

Up there by the winch, half buried in the snow, we shared in spirit the torment of his gradual ascent. The acoustics were such that we could hear the coffin grind against the rock, the hand-chain of the hoist clicking as it moved, the heavy breathing of the man who worked it. Every now and then he would joke or try to joke, and even sang to cheer himself and reassure his wife, who was with us at the winding-gear and showed high courage notwithstanding mortal anguish in her eyes.

The engineers, however, were more worried than any of us. They understood the machinery and just how little more it could endure. At any moment it might fail, or the cable snap, and then. . . . We guessed into what purgatory José's heart was plunged; for not one of us understood more clearly than did he how near Death was hovering.

At times there was despair in his exclamations and his laboured breathing. Even more pathetic was the voice of faith, when he suddenly called out in Basque the Psalmist's words: 'Lord, from the depths I cry to Thee!'

His journey had begun at 1 a.m. At 4 o'clock the nose of the container touched the under side of the balcony where Lépineux and Rossini stood waiting. It had taken three hours to climb 263 feet.

Bidegain shall now resume his story.

'My next job was to steer the coffin past the edge of this platform. The girder, leaning to my left, showed me what I must do. Thrusting all my weight on to the right guy-wire, I dragged the girder into position.

' "Up!" shouted Rossini into the telephone; and the container rose accordingly. The *pitons* were bending, and I wondered would they hold. At long last, however, my burden rested on the balcony: I had made it! Then I collapsed, exhausted but triumphant.'

Yes, he had brought the container so far; but at what cost! The next stage of the journey must soon begin—the most difficult of all, for from this point to the surface the great shaft is a mass of points and blades of rock.

Before the convoy could set out on the last length of its ascent, we had to bring Mauer up. He was still at −699; and I must confess that during the excitement of the last few hours he had been well-nigh forgotten. Lévi shouted to him, but there was no reply. It was a dreadful moment.

'Hullo, −263! Try to contact Mauer; he's not answering.'

Still there was no sound. Poor fellow, he had endured so long beneath those icy, pitiless cascades (against which he had unwisely failed to provide himself with waterproof clothing), that he was now half dead with cold. Bolted to the wall on a narrow ledge, he was in a state of prostration and practically unconscious. Aroused at length from his torpor, he was warned that the cable was on its way to pick him up; but it was repeatedly entangled or otherwise delayed, and took a very long time to reach him. Meanwhile, he suffered a relapse. Utterly exhausted and on the verge of desperation, he scarcely answered Lévi's frantic calls. . . . Eventually, however, at 7 a.m. he informed us that he had closed his snaphook on the cable and was ready to start. He was helped out of the shaft at 8:30 in a pitiful condition; but he had reached the bottom of the chasm, and held on through thick and thin.

Rossini came to the surface at 9 o'clock. Worn out, drenched to the skin, and numb with cold, he was assisted to his tent through a curtain of alternate rain and snow.

Apart from Brosset and Ballandraux (with whom for the moment we were not concerned, for they had turned in and were fast asleep in the Salle Lépineux) only two men remained in the shaft—Bidegain and Lépineux.

They were at −263, with the container tied down on the balcony; and there at about 9 a.m. a most extraordinary scene was enacted. These two bosom friends were heard over the telephone in acrimonious dispute. Lépineux was of the opinion that Bidegain had done more than his fair share and was in no condition to proceed. He wanted to take José's place and escort the container with the hoist. Bidegain protested that he was perfectly fit, and that in any case no one but himself knew how to handle the apparatus. José won the day. Lépineux agreed to be hauled up. His face bore the marks of extreme weariness, cold, and nervous tension.

The rest is briefly told; Bidegain completed the terrible ascent, locked in combat with his tragic burden; but the difficulties appeared to increase in proportion as his endurance ebbed away. The container was repeatedly held up by one obstacle after another.

'Up a yard! . . . Stop!' he would say into the microphone.
'Another yard! . . . Stop!'
'Down a yard! . . . Stop! . . .'

And so it went on, José striving desperately to release the coffin, steering it with his body while he worked the hoist. His hands were bleeding; he was in dreadful pain; but he moved like an automaton rising yard by yard, foot by foot, through that last stretch of calvary. Another would have given in; Bidegain fought on to the bitter end. Immediately he reached the surface he collapsed. It was 2 p.m. Twenty hours had elapsed since the coffin started on its journey, and Bidegain had done battle with it for thirteen of those hours.

Sauveur Bouchet, mayor of Licq-Athérey, and a team of powerful Basques lifted the container on to a sledge. They hauled it to the camp, where Fr. Attout said mass; and then the funeral cortège started for the valley. Drawn by a group of men straining at the ropes in face of a tremendous gale, the body of Loubens was borne away from Pierre Saint-Martin which he had loved so much and where he had laid down his life at the age of twenty-nine.

ARTHUR C. CLARKE

STATIONS IN SPACE

(From THE EXPLORATION OF SPACE. New York: Harper & Brothers, 1952)

The book from which I have taken this extract was published in 1951, and already instrument-carrying missiles, evisaged in it as a future possibility are in use. We have seen the launching of the first earth satellites, and no doubt, the space stations talked about here will soon be a reality. Man is by nature an explorer. There are few unexplored regions left on earth, so it is fortunate that the whole vast field of space exploration is before us.

Up above the world you fly,
Like a tea-tray in the sky.

Lewis Carroll—Alice in Wonderland

Many believe that the building of the space-station may be the first task of astronautics, antedating even the journey to the Moon. If one uses the word "space-station" to describe any artificial structure in a permanent, stable orbit, this view is certainly correct, for there is no doubt that instrument-carrying missiles will be established beyond the atmosphere at a fairly early date. Piloted missiles, remaining in their orbits for relatively short periods, will follow soon after. It is better, however, to restrict the term to permanent manned bases or observatories, constructed in space by materials ferried up by rocket and kept supplied with stores and personnel by the same means.

The idea of the space-station originally arose from the conception of orbital refuelling. When it was realized that

201

permanent structures could be established in space, it was
quickly seen that they would be useful for so many scientific
purposes that their employment as "filling stations" for rockets
might well become of secondary importance. Indeed, there
is probably no need to use space-stations at all for this purpose, at least in the earlier stages of interplanetary flight,
since the first spaceships will be refuelled directly from other
rockets. Not until there are large numbers of ships coming
and going at frequent intervals would it be worth while
setting up stations exclusively for refuelling purposes.

Let us briefly recall the underlying principles involved in
the creation of any form of artificial satellite. It will be remembered that, just outside the atmosphere, a body travelling horizontally at 18,000 m.p.h. would remain perpetually
in a stable, circular orbit, without requiring any power, and
making a complete rotation round the Earth in a little over
ninety minutes. At greater heights, the orbital speed needed
is less and so the period of revolution increases; 22,000 miles
above the surface the period is exactly 24 hours, and a body
here, if originally above the Equator, would revolve with the
Earth so that it would neither rise nor set. An object at a
greater distance would move more slowly than the Earth on
its axis and so would rise in the east and set in the west, as
do all the celestial bodies. Inside this limit of 22,000 miles a
satellite would rise in the *west* and set in the *east*, as does the
inner moon of Mars. (Anyone who cares to deduce from this
that the Martians are builders of space-stations is welcome
to do so!)

Bodies orbiting the Earth need not, however, travel on
circular paths: any ellipse with the centre of the Earth at
one focus is a possible orbit—so long, of course, as it does not
intercept the atmosphere. Nor need the orbits lie in the plane
of the Earth's own rotation: they could be at any angle to the

Equator, and could for example pass over the Poles. Which orbit was selected would depend on the purpose which the satellite was intended to fulfil.

A satellite a few hundred miles above the Equator would, because of the Earth's curvature, be visible only in a rather narrow band around the planet; and conversely, it would be able to survey only this restricted region. If its orbit passed over the Poles, however, the rotation of the planet would ensure that in quite a few revolutions of the satellite (i.e. in under a day) the whole surface of the Earth could be surveyed.

The same result would be obtained by using an orbit inclined to the Equator at an angle of, say 45 degrees, as long as the satellite was more than a thousand miles above the surface. Only the region immediately around the Poles would remain invisible from such a satellite in the course of 24 hours—although the distortion caused by the Earth's curvature, and the thickening atmospheric haze, would make useful observation impossible well before the station's visible "horizon" was reached.

Although, as is invariably the case, we shall not discover the full value of space-stations until we have actually constructed them, some of their uses are already obvious. The most important may be listed as follows: (1) astronomical and physical research; (2) meteorology and surveying; (3) biological studies; (4) refuelling; (5) radio relaying; and (6) dock facilities. Some of these functions could be carried out on the same station, but others demand such varying types of orbit that specialised stations would eventually have to be built, devoted to a single purpose. Thus the refuelling stations would be as near the Earth as possible (perhaps only five hundred miles up) whereas the astronomical ones would be at ten or a hundred times this distance. In this connection, however, it should be pointed out that it is much "cheaper," in terms of energy, to establish a close satellite than a distant one.

The advantages of a lunar observatory would apply still more strongly to an observatory in space, which would be able to survey the complete sphere of the sky. Even the Moon's extremely tenuous atmosphere might affect certain very delicate observations: this factor would not arise at all on the space-station.

Perhaps the most interesting possibility opened up by the space-station—although this is admittedly looking a long way ahead—is the fact that it would remove the restrictions imposed by gravity on the size of astronomical instruments. The great difficulties involved in building the 200-inch telescope on Mount Palomar were not primarily optical ones: they were largely due to the fact that the mirror and its auxiliaries had to remain rigid to a few millionths of an inch, no matter how the enormously heavy instrument was tilted and revolved.

In the weightless condition which always applies to a body in free orbit, the telescope structure need have only enough strength to maintain its stiffness. Indeed, the optical elements might be miles apart, if need be, with no physical connection at all. This would make it possible, for the first time, to build instruments which could measure the diameters of normal-sized stars. It might even become possible to detect planets of the nearer stars, something quite out of the question with earth-based equipment.

Since 1945, astronomers have become more and more interested in "telescopes" employing not light rays but radio waves, which have much greater penetrating power and so may be able to teach us something about the structure of parts of the Universe which we can never "see" in the ordinary way. Because radio waves are about a million times longer than light waves, it is necessary to build instruments of enormous size to get reasonable definition. The biggest radio-telescope yet built is over 200 feet in diameter (compared with 200 *inches* for the largest optical telescope) but even so its resolving power—that is, its ability to separate close objects—is thousands of times poorer than that of a pair of cheap opera-glasses. Moreover, because of its size, it is incapable of being moved.

Out in space, these limitations could be overcome, for it would be possible to build radio-telescopes literally miles in diameter—and still, thanks to their weightlessness, make them movable.

The assembly and operation of giant telescopes (optical or radio) floating in space clearly involves engineering problems of no mean order. Some of these will be considered on page 212 when we will discuss the actual construction of space-stations.

The opportunities which an artificial satellite would provide for physical research are equally great. A vast new field of experimental science would be opened up by the condition of weightlessness, and the presence of a virtually perfect vacuum of unlimited extent would be a stimulus to such studies as electronics, nuclear physics and the innumerable branches of technology which demand the use of low pressures. It would also be possible, for the first time, to produce temperatures not far from absolute zero over large volumes of space.

The study of cosmic rays (one of the key problems of modern physics) would receive an immense impetus, since only outside the atmosphere can we observe the primary radiations. Our knowledge of the ionosphere, which is of great practical importance in radio communication, would also advance rapidly once we were able to observe it from both sides.

Since a space-station a few thousand miles up would be able to survey the greater part of the planet in a couple of hours, watching all cloud formations and the movement of storm centres, it could clearly play a very valuable rôle in meteorology. Although ground stations would presumably still be necessary to fill in details of atmospheric pressure, temperature and so on, the satellite would be able to give the overall picture almost literally at a glance.

An orbital satellite (even one carrying no men or instruments) would also be invaluable as aid to navigation, provided that it was bright enough to be observed visually from the Earth. For centuries navigators have found their way over the surface of this planet by the use of sun, moon and stars. The existing heavenly bodies, however, are too far away for certain simple and direct position-finding methods to be employed, and one or two close satellites would greatly ease the problem.

The use of space-stations for biological research is a somewhat more speculative matter, for no one can say what medical science may discover from the study of organisms living for long periods under zero gravity. It is worth remembering that gravity is an important factor determining the possible size of micro-organisms (and indeed larger creatures). Its removal might produce some interesting results, though whether we could breed amœbæ as big as footballs remains to be seen!

The absence of gravity would certainly give medicine a most important new weapon, and not only for the treatment of obvious complaints like heart disease. It would probably accelerate any form of convalescence, and it is not too fantastic to suggest that many of the hospitals of the future will be found in space. We have seen that even the use of chemically fuelled rockets need not subject passengers to abnormally high or dangerous accelerations, so there is no reason why invalids should not travel in spaceships almost as safely as could people in normal health. (It is amusing to think that thirty years ago the idea of transporting the sick by air would have seemed complete madness—yet nowadays it is often the preferred method!) The fact that, apart from relatively short periods of eclipse by the Earth, a space-station would be in continuous sunlight would be of great therapeutic value. So would be the spectacle of the Earth itself, almost filling the sky and going through its phases from new to full in a few hours. The infinite variety of detail presented by the continents, seas and clouds, the pleasure of picking out familiar landmarks and even of observing the streets of the great cities through telescopes, should reconcile the patients to their temporary exile. The "Earthside" ward of a space-station hospital would, indeed, be a room with a view!

The refuelling and repair bases would probably be in the closest and hence most economical orbits. They might eventually become very extensive affairs—real "space-ports" with elaborate harbour facilities and huge hangars which could be pressurised to assist repair work. One would expect to find in them everything which a present-day seaport or airway terminus can provide.

Even when it becomes technically possible to make journeys to the other planets direct from the surface of the Earth, it seems doubtful if spaceships will in fact do so. The advantages of orbital techniques are so overwhelming that the time may never come (at least while the rocket is the only means of propulsion available) when interplanetary ships will take off from the Earth. The orbital space-ports may therefore expect a long period of useful service before they become technologically obsolete.

On a purely commercial basis, the greatest value of a space-station would probably arise from the radio and television services it could provide. An orbital satellite would make possible, for the first time, a reliable system of radio communication between all points on the Earth, irrespective of ionospheric conditions, magnetic storms, and all the other vicissitudes which plague long-distance radio. It would also vastly improve the quality of the service, for there would no longer be any need to rely on reflected waves with their subsequent distortions and interference. A direct beam service could link the station with any point on the hemisphere below, and messages could be relayed on to any other point around the curve of the planet—if necessary through a second space-station. Complete coverage of the whole Earth would be provided by three stations, revolving in the same orbit but spaced 120 degrees apart.

The obvious orbit for this purpose would be the 24-hour one, 22,000 miles above the Equator. Any point on the Earth's surface would then have at least one station permanently visible in the sky—and, moreover, *fixed* in the sky, unlike those wayward bodies the Sun, Moon and stars.

Perhaps the most exciting prospect raised by the relay chain is that it would make a world-wide system of television practicable. It is, indeed, almost impossible to imagine any other way in which this could be done, since the curve of the Earth limits the range of all surface transmitters, no matter how powerful, to less than a hundred miles. Three stations in space, linked to each other by microwave beams, could provide a television service *over the whole planet* for no more power than one of today's larger transmitters.

We have heard it said that it would be difficult to think of a better argument against space-travel than this. However, even if one takes a pessimistic view of television's cultural future, it should be pointed out that high-frequency waves of the type it uses have many other duties. They would make possible an almost unlimited number of interference-free communication channels, and would provide navigation and air safety services beyond anything in prospect today. A world society must possess a fast and reliable system of communications. The use of radio relays in space could provide this on a scale quite impossible by any other means, and at very great economy.

Shortly after the end of the Second World War, a good

deal was heard in the Press about gigantic "space-mirrors" which the Germans were supposed to be considering as weapons of war. The truth behind this rumour was somewhat less spectacular, as is usually the case. Twenty years earlier, Hermann Oberth had pointed out that it would be mechanically possible to build enormous mirrors in space by assembling sheets of metallic sodium on a spider's web of cables, kept rigid by its own rotation. A mirror two miles in diameter would collect about 10,000,000 h.p. of solar energy and if this were directed on the Earth beneath it could produce local heating over a fairly large area. Oberth imagined the use of such mirrors for weather control by the evaporation of water in some areas and the "directing" of the resultant vapour to others. The laws of optics would make it impossible to focus all the heat from such a mirror so accurately that it could be a really dangerous weapon, though if the mirror were made a good deal larger it might be able to make selected areas uncomfortably warm.

In any case, as a weapon the space-mirror must be regarded as obsolete before it has been built. We now know much more effective methods of incinerating populations, and the mirror itself would be an exceedingly vulnerable structure—it would take years to build yet could be destroyed in a few minutes by half a dozen guided missiles.

Although all the orbits hitherto mentioned have been circular, highly elliptical ones might be utilized for special purposes. These would take the station perhaps hundreds of thousands of miles away from the Earth and bring it back, a week or so later, to within a few hundred miles of the atmosphere.

It might be thought that the various orbits shown in the diagram would interfere with each other, and that there would be some danger of collisions. This, however, is quite impossible for the stations in circular orbits, which could not change their distances from the Earth without the use of power. Spaceships pulling away from the refuelling zone would, of course, have to time their departure to avoid passing too close to an outer station. Since there are so many billions of cubic miles involved, this would not be a serious restriction on flight orbits—which in any case would usually depart from the equatorial plane at quite short distances from Earth.

At least one complete book has already been written about the construction, planning and internal mechanics of space-stations. Here we can mention only a few of the more important aspects of this intriguing subject, which will certainly present the engineers of the future with some very peculiar problems.

The first stations will probably be built from spaceships that have been "cannibalized," to use a horrid but expressive word, once they have reached orbital velocity. The assembling of the structure will be done by men in space-suits, propelling themselves and their loads by reaction pistols or gas jets. Perhaps instead of what has now become the "conventional" space-suit, tiny one-man spaceships might be used, just large enough to hold a single occupant and fitted with the necessary handling mechanisms.

Relays of rockets would climb up into the orbit with loads of stores and structural materials and would simply "dump" their cargoes in space until they were needed. The assembling would of course be enormously simplified by the absence of gravity, and the first structure to be built would probably be a spherical chamber which could be pressurised to serve as living quarters for the space-station staff. From this beginning, endless variations of design are possible. Some stations might be in the shape of flat discs, slowly spinning so that there would appear to be normal gravity at the rim. At the axis there would be no gravity at all, so in the one station it would be possible for the staff to live normal lives yet carry out zero-gravity experiments whenever they wished. Other satellites—particularly those used for astronomical research, where instruments have to be kept rigidly fixed for long periods in an unvarying direction—would have no rotation. The crews might live when off duty in an associated spinning station a few miles away, transferring from one to the other by low-powered rockets.

Over the years and centuries the stations would grow by a process of accretion as new chambers and laboratories were built, until they might eventually become miles in extent forming a loosely connected group of structures serving many different purposes—in fact, veritable cities in space. The larger ones would be easily visible from the Earth as bright stars crossing the sky rapidly from west to east, but often vanishing for a while as they passed into the shadow of the planet and were "eclipsed."

Although it has been assumed that, once set revolving in its orbit, an artificial satellite would continue to circle the Earth for ever with clorkwork precision, this is not perfectly correct. The disturbing effect of the Sun and Moon, and the attraction of the Earth's own equatorial bulge, would slowly alter the orbit of a satellite, causing its plane of rotation to precess or tilt slowly up and down. The effect is very small and in most cases would not be of any practical importance. It would always be possible to readjust an orbit, if necessary, by the use of minute amounts of rocket power. Indeed, some care would have to be taken to prevent accidental "perturbations" of the orbit when waste material was ejected from the station or fresh stores were taken aboard.

No doubt with the further development of astronautics artificial satellites will be built elsewhere than near the Earth. Often there would be existing asteroids or small moons which might provide a foundation on which to work and could also supply much of the necessary structural material. In this case, there would be little distinction between a space-station and a planetary colony.

Although orbital bases circling the planets might be built for numerous reasons, many might travel on independent orbits around the Sun and would thus be artificial planets rather than artificial satellites. One obvious use for such bases would be in connection with interplanetary communication. It would fairly often happen that a spaceship or a planet would be on the far side of the Sun from Earth and so out of touch by direct transmission. A space-station moving in the Earth's orbit, but some scores of millions of miles from our planet, could be used as a repeater or relay and so would enable us to "see round the Sun."

The laws of celestial mechanics show that a small body could travel in the Earth's orbit in this fashion if it formed an equilateral triangle with the Earth and the Sun. There are two positions where this is possible—one 93,000,000 miles "behind" the Earth and the other the same distance ahead of it. Similar stable positions exist in the orbits of the other planets: in the case of Jupiter they are already occupied by two groups of asteroids known as the "Trojans."

If we take the long view of humanity's future, the time may come when these artificial worlds may be as important as the original, natural planets. In his book *The World, The Flesh and The Devil* (one of the most astonishing flights of controlled scientific imagination ever made) Professor J. D. Bernal has taken this idea to what must surely be its ultimate conclusions. He imagines spherical planetoids many miles in diameter, with food-producing areas immediately beneath the transparent outer skin. Lower still would be the machines which regulated temperature and air—which controlled, in other words, the climate of the little world.

The central volume would be the living region, which, because of the absence of gravity, would be much roomier than we, with our flat, "two-dimensional" outlook, can easily imagine. As Bernal points out, "a globe interior eight miles across would contain as much effective space as a countryside one hundred and fifty miles square even if one gave a liberal allowance of air, say fifty feet above the ground."

These worlds might develop their own cultures and specialised activities, though they would be in constant touch with their neighbours and with the various planetary civilisations. It is even possible that, eventually, only a small proportion of the human race would live upon the original planets of the Sun. A thousand years from now, indeed, the Sun's family may be very much more numerous than it is today.

INDEX

Santa Clara County
LIBRARY

Renewals:

(800) 471-0991